How to Understand Hinduism

Jean-Christophe Demariaux

How to Understand Hinduism

SCM PRESS LTD

Translated by John Bowden from the French *Pour Comprendre l'Hindouisme*, published 1995 by Les Editions du Cerf, 29 boulevard Latour Maubourg, Paris.

© Les Éditions du Cerf 1995

Translation © John Bowden 1995

All rights reserved. No part of this publication may be reproduced, stored in a retrieval system, or transmitted, in any form or by any means, electronic, mechanical, photocopying, recording or otherwise, without the prior written permission of the publishers, SCM Press Ltd.

Nihil obstat: Father Anton Cowan
Censor
Imprimatur: Monsignor Thomas Egan, V.G.
24th October, 1995.

The *Nihil obstat* and *Imprimatur* are a declaration that a book or pamphlet is considered to be free from doctrinal or moral error. It is not implied that those who have granted the *Nihil obstat* and *Imprimatur* agree with the contents, opinions or statements expressed.

---

0 334 02622 9

First British edition published 1995
by SCM Press Ltd,
9–17 St Albans Place, London N1 0NX

Typeset at The Spartan Press Ltd, Lymington, Hants
and printed in Great Britain by
Redwood Books, Trowbridge, Wiltshire

Contents

Introduction — vii

Part One
Vedic Religion — 1

Prologue — 3

I The Vedic Literature: The Veda — 7

    1. The Samhitas — 8
    2. The Brahmanas — 8
    3. The Aranyakas — 9
    4. The Upanishads — 9

II Indo-European Mythology and the Vedic Pantheon — 11

    1. The major features of the pantheon — 13
    2. Two sovereign gods, Mitra and Varuna — 14
    3. A warrior god, Indra — 16
    4. Two 'liturgical' gods, Agni and Soma — 17
    5. Other gods — 19

III Vedic Beliefs, Speculations and Rites — 23

    1. Cosmogony — 23
    2. Eschatology — 25
    3. *Brahman* and *atman* — 27
    4. Vedic ceremonies and rites — 29

Part Two
From Vedism to Hinduism — 37

I The New Literary Sources — 39

1. The post-Vedic Upanishads and the Dharma Shastras — 41
2. Epic literature: the Mahabharata and the Ramayana — 43
3. Puranic literature and the Tantras — 49

II Hindu Myths, Beliefs and Rites — 52

1. A renewed pantheon — 53
2. The speculative framework — 72
3. Hindu rites and festivals — 79
4. Historical perspectives — 86

III Hinduism in the Modern World — 89

1. Reform movements and contemporary 'masters' — 89
2. The advent of gurus in the West — 101
3. The promise of 'inter-faith' dialogue: the experience of Dom Le Saux — 106

Conclusion — 110

The Indian Union (simplified administrative map) — 113
For Further Reading — 114
List of Boxes — 116
List of Illustrations — 117
Index and Glossary — 118

Introduction

The term 'Hinduism', commonly used in the Western world to denote the wide range of beliefs, practices and cults of 'Hindu religion', is a recent invention. It was coined by Europeans in the first half of the nineteenth century, at a time when the social and religious structures of India still escaped the wisdom of the first historians of religions. 'Hindu', like 'Hindu-ism', is derived from the Sanskrit term *sindhu*, meaning 'river' or 'water-course'; it is also used to denote the great river Indus in north-west India, which today irrigates Pakistan. Transcribed *hindu* in Persian under the Achaemenids, the word *sindhu* denoted the area through which the Indus (the Sind of the Muslim era) flowed and also its inhabitants, and then, by extension, the whole of the Indian sub-continent and its mosaic of peoples. The word *hindu*, taken up and Hellenized by the Greeks as *hindia*, was ultimately to provide the present name of the sub-continent, India, in European languages.

Following the Muslim invasions of India and the invaders' custom of using the Persian term 'Hindu-stan' to denote India – 'Land of Hindu' or 'Land of the Hindus' – and 'Hindu' to denote the indigenous population which did not practise Islam, the word *hindu* took on a religious connotation, since from an Islamic perspective it covered all the inhabitants of India who were neither Muslims nor Buddhists. It was only from the sixteenth century that the first Europeans who landed on the coast of India distinguished the 'Indians' from the 'Hindus', the former term referring to the secular sphere and the latter to the world of religion.

Usually understood in a very general sense, the term 'Hinduism' was then used in the West to designate 'Hindu religion' *en bloc* in order to distinguish it from the other religions which emerged from Indian soil, like Buddhism, Jainism and the Sikh religion.

A historical approach to 'Hindu religion' tends to restrict the use of this term to the religious forms which came after those of the Vedic period. In discussing the

Vedic period proper (between the fourteenth and the fourth centuries BCE), it is customary to use the terms 'Vedism' or 'the religion of the Vedas'. The term 'Brahmanism' is sometimes used as a synonym for 'Hinduism' in a general sense, but more particularly it is kept as a description for the post-Vedic phase of 'Hindu religion'. This is characterized on the one hand by the generalization of the notion of Brahman (the impersonal Absolute) and on the other by the growing importance of the priestly caste of Brahmins within Indian society. However, it is difficult to say at precisely what period the move from 'Brahmanism' to 'Hinduism' takes place. It seems that the beginnings of the Hindu synthesis coincide with the appearance of the epic literature (between the fourth and second centuries BCE).

In Hinduism, the notion of *dharma*, which is so rich in content, denotes the normal and natural disposition of beings and things, the idea or a social and cosmic order, the moral and religious norm to which every 'Hindu' has to conform in accordance with the attributes of his condition, his age, his caste. The notion of *dharma* is so important in the Hindu universe that this term has come to denote Hinduism itself by means of two expressions: *santana dharma*, the 'eternal law', and *varna ashrama dharma*, the 'law of castes and ages of life'. For every Hindu in the first three castes (*varna*), self-realization is a matter of fully accomplishing one's 'own *dharma*' (*svadharma*) along the four stages (*ashramas*) of the ideal Indian life: a period of study (*brahmacharya*) under the authority of a master, a period of family life (*garhasthya*), a period of retreat and contemplation (*vanaprastha*) once the children have grown up, and a stage of renunciation and eremitic life (*sannyas*).

Furthermore, Hindu tradition has specified the four 'goals of human life' (*purushartha*). It first distinguishes the group of the 'three worldly values' (*trivarga*), around which a person organizes his life: *kama*, the fulfilment of legitimate desire; *artha*, the idea of self-realization in the social and material sphere; and *dharma*, the idea of duty which also embraces a social ethic. *Moksha*, deliverance, completing and transcending this triad of values, is about spiritual realization and the means of escaping the cycle of rebirth *(samsara)*.

The discovery of 'Hindu religion' by the West is relatively recent. Without exaggerating, one could say that up to the end of the eighteenth century there was only scant and fragmentary information in Europe about the great religious and philosophical systems of India. Before coming to the information essential for understanding the main features of Hindu religious thought, it is useful to look at the main stages of this discovery.

Orientalism came to the universities at the end of the eighteenth century, in the period of social and political revolutions which soon embraced all Europe. In the space of about fifty years, philologists, linguists and historians of religion were to open up all the doors of the East to Europe, bringing about a real cultural revolution on the old continent. India very quickly came to occupy a central place in this rearrangement of cultures, since Sanskrit appeared to be both the original language of humanity (the fantasy of the mother tongue) and a common parent of Latin and Greek.

The first publications on Indology enjoyed considerable success among the European intelligentsia, especially in Germany and France. They influenced the thought of Arthur Schopenhauer and, among the German Romantics, particularly Friedrich Schlegel.

The birth of the Theosophical Society in 1875 marks the beginning of a second period. At this time its founders, Colonel Henry Steel Olcott (1832–1907) and the medium Helena Petrovna Blavatsky (1831–1891), stated quite explicitly that, disappointed in all their attempts to acquire the knowledge they sought under other horizons, they were turning their gaze towards the East, the source of all religious and philosophical systems. In 1882 the headquarters of the society was transferred from New York to the Adyar district of Madras, where it is still located today. This implantation on Indian soil has allowed the society to acquire a large number of original Indian manuscripts and to create one of the richest libraries in the country.

The doctrine propagated by the movement never got beyond the stage of a pseudo-philosophical syncretism combining a series of doctrinal elements taken from Buddhism and Hinduism with disparate elements drawing on the world of occultism and parapsychology, to which were added notions of evolution and progress. However, despite the caricature which this movement has made of traditional Hindu doctrine, there is no denying the fact that in the West, and particularly in the Anglo-Saxon world, the Theosophical Society and its dissident branches have played a major role in spreading and handing down a terminology which can convey Eastern conceptions and which today still constitutes the creed of an enormous variety of groups, usually summed up under the label 'new age'. It is in this way, and in this way alone, that it has contributed to making Hindu thought known in the West.

This second phase also saw the creation in Europe and the United States of societies for studying Vedantic thought affiliated to the Ramakrishna Mission (1897), which was founded in Calcutta by one of the first Swamis (literally 'master'), Swami Vivekananda (1863–1902). He made the message of India known in the West. In September 1893, on the occasion of the Parliament of the World's Religions organized jointly by the Presbyterian Church of Chicago and the Catholic hierarchy of the United States, Swami Vivekananda gave a remarkable speech and bore witness by his presence to the vitality of Hinduism. The Parliament of the World's Religions, which today stands out as the first encounter of religions at a planetary level, is also the starting point of the missionary work of the Hinduism of the gurus in the West whom we shall be meeting later in this book.

PART ONE

Vedic Religion

Prologue

The civilization of the Indus valley has proved one of the major archaeological discoveries of the twentieth century. Two great urban centres, the cities of Harappa in the Punjab and Mohenjo-Daro in the Sind, mark the end of a long development. Uncovered at the beginning of the 1920s by the excavations of Sir John Marshall and Rakhal Das Banerji, in the middle of the third millennium BCE these cities flourished at the heart of a vast territory extending more than seven hundred miles from north to south and almost four hundred miles from east to west. They represent the first urban civilization on the sub-continent of India and Pakistan. The golden age of this civilization (between 2300 and 2100 BCE) is contemporaneous with the period of Akkad in Mesopotamia, a region with which it had maritime commercial relations. Its decline and sudden disappearance are an enigma which has caused much argument and still has not been completely resolved. For a long time it was believed that the civilization of the Indus had succumbed to the 'Aryan' invasions, but these invasions have proved to be later than its decline; at the very least, this culture had already declined by the time that the first waves of invaders arrived in India. It has been argued that a combination of factors contributed to its disappearance, including a change in the water supply as a result of deforestation, and devastating floods. However, recent research suggests a less dramatic explanation. The civilization of Harappa

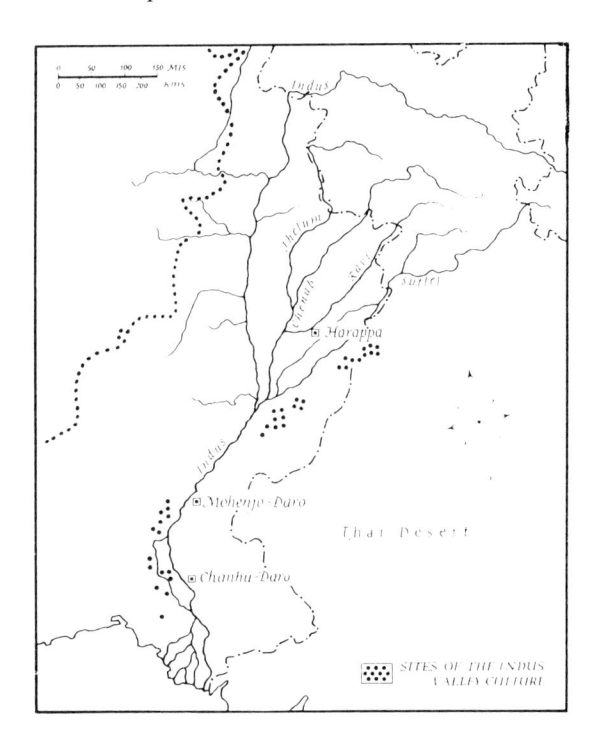

1. The Indus valley, showing the centres of Harappa and Mohenjo-Daro

may have disappeared as a result of a fragmentation and regionalization which began at the end of the third millennium and led to the appearance of a series of distinct geographical entities. This development was also accompanied by an agricultural revolution (the introduction of summer cereal crops and new kinds of animals: donkeys, camels and horses), which by around 1800 BCE had led to the establishment of a stable rural economy.

2. Terracotta statuette of female deity from the Indus valley

Although no specifically religious buildings have been excavated, archaeological exploration has revealed some characteristics of the religion of the Indus valley. However, because it has proved impossible to decipher the writing of this civilization, the main features are not known. Female clay figures found on the site of Mohenjo-Daro probably bear witness to the cult of a 'mother goddess'. On the basis of a thesis formulated by Sir John Marshall, the effigy of a male deity with three faces, seated in a yogic posture and surrounded by animals, represented on steatite seals, has often been interpreted as a prototype of the God Shiva (under his form Pasupati, 'lord of the beasts'). However, this is by no means certain. On the other hand, the discovery of several cemeteries at Harappa has provided information about types of burial. The 'great bath' in the upper city (the 'citadel') of Mohenjo-Daro may have been used for cultic ablutions.

3. 'Lord of the beasts'

It is no longer possible to determine the original homeland of the 'Aryan' populations (this term is used for convenience, but it should not suggest the existence of an Indo-European race, since 'Indo-European' is a strictly linguistic term) which invaded the plains of eastern Iran, Asia Minor and Mesopotamia, and north-west India at the beginning of the second millennium BCE. In the nineteenth century their starting point was located on the plain of the Pamir; today there is general agreement that it was on the great Russian plain, perhaps in southern Russia between the Volga and the Dniepr. These conquerors had mastered the art of war to a remarkable degree. The domestication of the horse made it possible for them to develop a particularly effective chariot force. Moreover, they

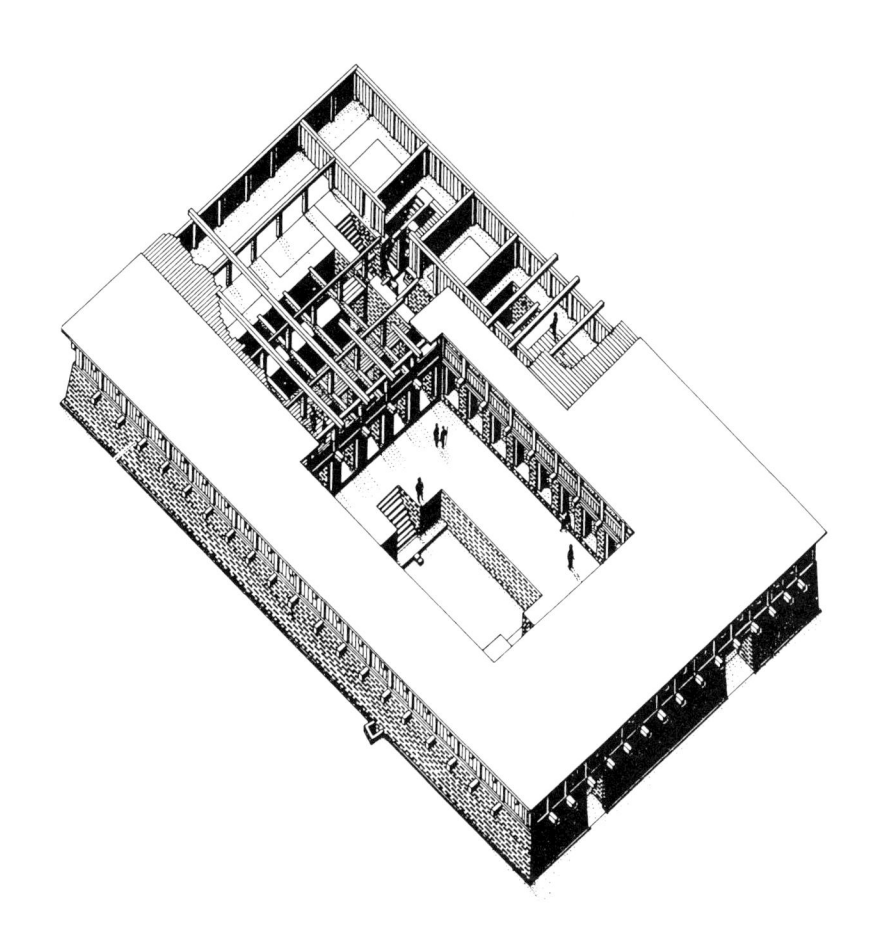

4. The 'great bath' of Mohenjo-Daro, with ancillary buildings (reconstruction)

had a profoundly original social and religious structure which was their common denominator. This consisted of a hierarchy arranged by spheres of activity and a distribution of tasks on a threefold model (control of magic and religion, war and production) which was matched in society by three functional 'castes' or 'classes': the priests, the military, and the craftsmen or producers.

These newcomers, who reached the Indus by the Punjab at a time when the civilization of the Indus was in decline or perhaps already in ruins, belonged to an Indo-Iranian branch which had probably become detached from the common Indo-European stem in the third millennium. They ended by imposing their way of life and beliefs on India as far as the plain of the Ganges (around 800 BCE). Certain texts of Vedic literature give us some information about the 'Aryan' presence in India. They mention battles between the 'Aryan' tribes, but equally the battles between these and the Dasas or Dasyus, who have sometimes been identified with the indigenous people of the north-west Indus.

The 'Aryans' of the Indus had a linguistic affinity

with their brothers settled in Iran. This indicates a common origin which can be found, for example, in the name of their gods. Moreover, they called themselves by the same expression denoting 'noble (man)', in India *arya* (Sanskrit) and in Iran *airya* (Avestic), hence the English 'Aryan'.

These first Indo-European migrations were followed by other waves (Celts, Germans, Hellenes, Italiots, Slavs), which over the centuries allowed the Indo-Europeans to become masters of a vast territory covering an area extending from Ireland to the Gulf of Bengal and from Scandinavia to Greece. This was a phenomenon quite without parallel, and was of tremendous importance for the history of humankind.

5. Bull found on a seal from Mohenjo-Daro

I
The Vedic Literature: The Veda

The Vedic period lasted for more than a millennium, between the fourteenth and the fourth century BCE. It can be said to comprise the centuries during which, from the Indus in the north-west, the 'Aryan' invaders imposed their language (Sanskrit) and their religion on northern India. However, if the dominant element of Vedic religion is part of the cultural universe of the 'Aryans', as the Veda testifies, it is certain that the whole Hindu religious tradition dos not draw its origins from a single source which could be counted the culture of the invaders. The cult of the phallus (*sisna*), the mythology of the snake gods (*nagas*) and the genies (*yakshas*), along with the great god Shiva of classical Hinduism, have pre-Aryan origins, which in all probability are Dravidian. Furthermore, there may well be some affinity between the 'mother goddess' of Mohenjo-Daro and the figure of the goddess (Devi) known in Hinduism under very different forms, notably those of Durga or Kali, and also of the many 'village deities' (*gramadevatas*).

Since there are no religious monuments from the Vedic period, the only real source of information we have for understanding the religion of this period is the sacred literature. By analysing the content of the hymns, treatises and liturgical commentaries of the Veda, we can understand the structure of the pantheon, the cultic practices, the beliefs and speculations of Vedism. However, it is important to note that the Veda does not give the whole religious message of ancient India. It represents only the 'Aryan' clans, and consequently excludes popular religion and the religious forms characteristic of the indigenous populations.

The term 'Veda' – etymologically derived from the Sanskrit root *vid-*, 'know' – denotes a literary body the composition of which extends over almost a millennium, between 1400 and 500 BCE. Developed within 'Aryan' priestly families, this body of texts produced in 'Vedic' Sanskrit represents, as the etymology emphasizes, sacred knowledge *par excellence*, since the non-human origin and the eternity of the Veda leave no room for doubt. It is in fact said that this divine science was breathed out by the Absolute (Brahman) and revealed by 'audition' (*sruti*) to a number of eminent sages (*rishis*) who, having received it directly by audition, then transmitted it from generation to generation through a long chain of masters and disciples. The Veda is still *the* eternal word (*vach*), the quintessence of the world as sound, to such a degree that from speculations on a sound, a word or a phrase a philosophy of knowledge through the word and a metaphysic of sound emerged which the Tantric schools would later develop to an unprecedented degree.

The Vedic texts which have come down to us are divided into schools (literally 'branch', *sakha*). They seem to have been four in number and to have been connected with the four types of officiating priests responsible for the ceremonies of the Vedic cult. Though there are several recensions of the Veda, it is nevertheless fundamentally one: the different recensions of the same text simply remind us that the Veda has not been compiled in a rigorous way according to a predetermined plan.

The *sruti* (root *sru*, 'hear', literally 'that which is heard') form the totality of direct testimonies handed down by the ancient *rishis*. They are embodied in the Veda, the compilation of which is traditionally attributed to the mythic Vedavyasa (literally, the 'compiler of the Vedas'), who is also believed to have been the head of a group of important sages.

In this complex body, a distinction is made between four collections (*samhitas*) which constitute what is sometimes called the Four Vedas (*chaturveda*).

1. The Samhitas

1. The **Rig Veda Samhita** (literally the 'Veda of the strophes') contains 1028 hymns (*suktas*) of unequal length divided into ten 'books' (literally 'circles', *mandalas*), giving a total of more than ten thousand strophes (*riks*). This is the earliest part of the Veda (between the twelfth and the tenth centuries BCE). The vast majority of these hymns are praises addressed to the main deities (Agni, Indra, Soma, Varuna) or descriptions of the foundation myths (the birth of the world, the primordial sacrifice). Other hymns with a mythical theme have been composed in dialogue form. It is possible that these belonged to larger compositions mixing prose and verse, of which only the verse part remains today.

The 'Veda of the strophes' is the sphere reserved to the priest (*hotr*), who, in the solemn cult, is charged with invoking the gods by the recitation of hymns.

2. The **Yajur Veda Samhita** (literally the 'Veda of sacrificial formulae') contains all the formulae (*yajus*) necessary for completing the sacrifice, which were recited by the *adhvaryu*, an officiant specializing in magical formulae. Written in prose and verse, it has been preserved in two versions: of the first, called the 'white' (*sukla*) Yajur Veda, there is only a single collection (the Vajasaneyi Samhita), but of the second, called the black (*krishna*) Yajur Veda, there are four.

3. The **Sama Veda Samhita** (literally the 'Veda of the melodies') has come down to us in three different recensions. This Samhita contains almost two thousand strophes, most taken from the Rig Veda and accompanied by musical notations intended for the *udgatr*, the officiant who specialized in performing melodies (*saman*).

4. The **Atharva Veda Samhita** (literally the 'Veda of Atharvan', the name of a family of Vedic priests), divided into twenty 'sections' (*kandas*) and edited in verse and prose, has hymns in one part and in the other a collection of formulae and magical recipes (charms for love and long life, talismans against sickness or demon-possession, incantations against the demons).

However, this fourth Samhita does not have the same spiritual authority as the other three, which traditionally constitute the 'threefold science' (*trayi vidya*), that is, knowledge in the form of strophe (*rik*), sacrificial formula (*yajus*) and melody (*saman*). Moreover, this fourth Samhita attained the rank of the fourth Veda only at a late stage.

2. The Brahmanas

The Vedic literature of the cycle of 'revelation' (*sruti*) is extended in a second category of probably later texts (between the tenth and the seventh centuries BCE), the Brahmanas (literally 'interpretation of Brahman', in other words here the mystical power which maintains the universe and is renewed in sacrifice). These voluminous treatises in prose contain prescriptions about the performance of sacrifices and explanations of the meaning of ritual, which refer to a surprising and prodigious series of parallels between the myths and liturgy. The Brahmanas are not so much concerned with how ritual is done as with why it is done, and any technical details given are the occasion for explaining doctrine. The basis of the thought of the Brahmanas is that sacrifice is effective only if the ritual is observed down to the smallest detail. The sacrifice has become an end in itself which goes so far as to eclipse the power of the Vedic gods, since their power seems subordinate to sacrifice. However, it should be noted that in certain passages of the Brahmanas there are the beginnings of a strictly philosophical thought, even if this is far from being detached from the millstone of ritual and the framework of religious formulations.

This exegetical literature, some texts of which have unfortunately been lost, has often come down to us through a series of recensions corresponding to many different priestly schools. So it is that the Rig Veda has two Brahmanas; the 'white' Yajur Veda one (the famous Satapatha Brahmana, the 'Brahmana of the Hundred Ways'); and the 'black' Yajur Veda one; the Sama Veda has two major Brahmanas and seven minor ones; and the Atharva Veda has just one.

3. The Aranyakas

The Aranyakas (literally 'forest [texts]') are esoteric and mystical treatises attached to the Brahmanas, of which they are supplements. Their name recalls that they were studied in a limited circle in the solitude of the forest (*aranya*) since, it seems, they relate to esoteric truths (*rahasaya*) and concern developments relating to the symbolic interpretation of rites or the mention of terrifying deities. Several types of text are covered by this single title. Alongside texts relating to the transmission of particularly secret teachings and theological commentaries analogous to those included in the Brahmanas, there are also some speculative passages, radically modifying reflection on sacrifice (the interiorization of sacrifice). These texts of a new kind announce the end of the world-view of Vedic ritualism and open the way to the Upanishads, which deepen the process of the interiorization of sacrifice, stating that deliverance (*moksha*) is obtained, not by ritual works but by an intuitive knowledge of a metaphysical kind (*jnana*), which alone can unveil the structures of the real. Compared with all the other texts of the Vedas (Brahmanas), which represent the 'section about actions' (*karma-kanda*), the literature of the Aranyakas and the Upanishads represents the 'section about knowledge' (*jnana-kanda*).

4. The Upanishads

The last literary stratum of the cycle of the *sruti*, the Upanishads – the etymology of the term seems to denote 'equivalence' (esoteric) or 'connection' – forms a group of around 250 treatises. These are generally brief (a few pages long), and their often elliptical content is concerned with the identification of mystical connections or equivalences between human beings and the universe. This doctrine of correspondences between the microcosm and the macrocosm culminates in the supreme connection summed up in the formula *tat tvam asi*, 'You are That', of the Chandogya Upanishad (VI, 8–11), which denotes the identity between *atman*, the internal supra-subjective and immortal self (the soul in Western language) and Brahman, the transpersonal Absolute, the 'one with no second' (*ekam evadvitiyam*), in other words the ultimate reality of things (see pp. 30–1 below).

The Upanishads traditionally constitute the Veda-anta = Vedanta, literally the 'end of the Veda', an expression which should also be understood to denote the doctrinal conclusion of the Veda, since these texts which come after the collections of hymns (Samhitas) and commentaries on the Veda (Brahmanas) depart from the mystique of sacrifice to develop a metaphysical doctrine which was to serve as a philosophical basis for the conceptions of later Hinduism. Only fourteen Upanishads

The Vedic Upanishads

The fourteen Upanishads from the Vedic period (sixth-third century BCE), with the corresponding Vedic collection (p = prose; v = verse)

Brihadaranyaka Upanishad	(p)	'White' Yajur Veda
Chandogya Upanishad	(p)	Sama Veda
Aitareya Upanishad	(p)	Rig Veda
Kausitaki Upanishad	(p)	Rig Veda
Taittiriya Upanishad	(p)	'Black' Yajur Veda
Kena Upanishad	(p and v)	Sama Veda
Isha Upanishad	(v)	'White' Yajur Veda
Katha Upanishad	(v)	'Black' Yajur Veda
Mantra Upanishad	(v)	'Black' Yajur Veda
Mahabarayana Upanishad	(p and v)	'Black' Yajur Veda
Mundaka Upanishad	(v)	Atharva Veda
Prasna Upanishad	(p and v)	Atharva Veda
Mandukya Upanishad	(p)	Atharva Veda
Maitrayani Upanishad	(p)	'Black' Yajur Veda

go back to the Vedic period. All the others are of later date, some even having been written in the modern period.

The texts of the *sruti* do not constitute the whole of Vedic literature. As well as this enormous corpus there are the *smrti* (root *smr*, 'remember', literally 'memory'), which represent the totality of sacred texts retained in and transmitted by memorized tradition; however, these are in harmony with the texts of the original revelation (*sruti*). This literature, which largely overflows the framework of the Vedic period (it was codified only at the beginning of the Christian era), contains the epics (Mahabharata and Ramayana), the collections of traditional Indian law (Dharma Shastras) and the Puranas. Among the Vedic texts belonging to this cycle we find those of the Veda-anga = Vedangas (literally 'members of the Veda'), a term which denotes all the texts relating to the six sciences attached to the Veda. These sciences facilitate the understanding of the Vedic texts and are *siksha* (phonetics), *kalpa* (ritual), *vyakarana* (grammar), *nirukta* (etymology), *chandas* (measure) and *jyotisha* (astronomy).

II
Indo-European Mythology and the Vedic Pantheon

Research into Indo-European religion began in the nineteenth century in the sphere of comparative linguistics, which showed that the various branches of the Indo-European languages (Celtic, Germanic, Hellenic, Indo-Iranian, Romano-Italic and Slav) represent different degrees of development of a common original stem. The twentieth century then saw a crucial development, particularly thanks to the work of Georges Dumézil (1898–1986). His work on comparative mythology, based on a detailed analysis of a vast amount of literature (Vedic hymns, Indian epics [the Mahabharata], Mazdaean religious texts, Latin historical and religious texts and Icelandic sagas), brought out the agreements between these mythologies, which related not so much to the identity of the stories in them as to their structure, which was based on a 'tripartite functionalism': control of magic and religion, war, and production. In Roman mythology this threefold pattern is illustrated by the trinity of Jupiter, Mars and Quirinus and in the Germanic universe by the group Odin, Thor and Freyr. In the Vedic pantheon the 'first function' is duplicated in two complementary tendencies: Varuna represents magical and religious sovereignty and Mitra juridical sovereignty. The 'second function', which is also duplicated, falls to Indra, the invincible god, who guides the 'Aryan' tribes and represents just and controlled warlike force, and Vayu, who embodies brute force. The 'third function' associated with fertility and work pertains to the Nasatya twins, also known as the Asvins (*Asvini devatas*).

The ideology of three functions can also be found in certain cultural practices which have a threefold pattern in these societies (three types of marriage, of medicine or of expiation). They can equally be found in the three functional 'classes' or 'castes' which make up the framework of certain Indo-European societies, notably among the Indo-Iranians and the Celts. In India, according to the ideal Vedic model, the class of Brahmins (sacrificing priests), entrusted with the administration of the sacred, thus performs the 'first function'. The class of Kshatriyas (military nobility and warriors), entrusted with the protection of society, performs the 'second function'. The class of the Vaishyas (cattle-breeders, farmers, merchants), responsible for production, performs the 'third function', which also comprises notions of material riches, pleasure and fertility. The members of these three high classes are the only ones who can bear the name Aryans. They are also called *dvija*, i.e. 'twice-born'. The fourth class, which is thought to be inferior and is excluded from the rites of Arya society, namely the Shudras or serfs, traditionally has a servant role. It is possible that the very

The Three Social Functions and the Caste System

The works of Brahmins, Kshatriyas, Vaishyas and Shudras are different, in harmony with the three powers of their born nature.

The works of a Brahmin are peace; self-harmony, austerity and purity; loving-forgiveness and righteousness; vision and wisdom and faith.

These are the works of a Kshatriya: a heroic mind, inner fire, constancy, resourcefulness, courage in battle, generosity and noble leadership.

Trade, agriculture and the rearing of cattle is the work of a Vaishya. And the work of the Shudra is service.

They all attain perfection when they find joy in their work.

A man attains perfection when his work is worship of God, from whom all things come and who is in all.

(Bhagavad Gita XVIII, 41–45)

Caste

A social system established in India by the Aryans, probably at first determined by a man's occupation. With the passing of centuries caste became hereditary and was surrounded by many restrictions designed to prevent caste-mixture. Those belonging to the lowest stratum of Hindu society, called Untouchables, were considered outside the caste system. They were originally excluded for their primitive and outlandish socio-religious customs, a practice which later became hereditary. As described in the Gita, the idea of caste refers to a natural order. The four main castes are: 1. the Brahmin caste (priests, pandits, philosophers, religious leaders); 2. the Kshatriya caste (politicians, military men, persons of royal descent); 3. the Vaishya caste (providers, a category which includes merchants, farmers and artisans); and 4. the Shudra caste (labourers and servants). In this sense the castes are necessary components of human society. The Gita teaches that by performing his caste duty as worship of God, each man can transcend caste and reach the spiritual perfection which is his birthright.

(from *A Brief Dictionary of Hinduism*, Vedanta Society)

existence of this fourth 'class' is the remote recollection of indigenous populations who were subjected by the invaders at the time of the conquest.

Most of the hymns of the Rig Veda are hymns of praise addressed to deities belonging to a very wide pantheon which is complex both in terms of the number of its gods and their internal harmony. Furthermore, not all the Vedic texts agree on the distribution of the pantheon, because of the long course of their development, which necessarily reflects the religious evolution of Vedism.

When Vedic people invoke a particular deity, that becomes the highest and most important deity in the pantheon and takes on the attributes of the other gods. This conception of divinity, which makes the gods interchangeable as a result of a permutation of their attributes, blurred the structure of the pantheon to such a degree that one of the founders of the comparative study of religion, F. Max Müller (1823–1900), had to coin a word to denote this conception. He spoke of 'henotheism'. Influenced by a number of Romantic conceptions, Müller explained that at the origins of humanity religion emerged from a sense of dependence and an intuitive perception of the deity which did not imply either unity (monotheism) or plurality (polytheism), but simply indicated a degree of oneness.

1. The major features of the pantheon

The Rig Veda (I, 139, 11) gives the number of thirty-three gods, distinguished by their usual area of residence. There are those who dwell in the empyrean, those who live in the airy regions, and those who spend their days on earth, eleven gods in each group. However, we must give up any hope of listing these thirty-three gods, since the Rig Veda does not distinguish them all systematically. Another passage (IX, 29, 24) in the same collection counts thirty gods. In these two texts, the numbers thirty and thirty-three are clearly symbolic and convey the ideas of both multitude and perfection. They can also be found in various forms in other texts. Thus in a famous passage from the earliest of the Vedic Upanishads, the Brihadaranyaka Upanishad (III, 9, 1), the *rishi* Yajnavalkya reduces the number of gods from the numbers 303 and 3,003 to just one. Similarly, modern Hinduism reckons thirty-three *kotis* of deities (1 *koti* = 10 millions), a hyperbolic form of the number provided by the Vedas. Later, and particularly in the Brahmanas, the thirty-three gods of the pantheon are subdivided into twelve Adityas, eleven Rudras, eight Vasus and two Asvins, the two latter sometimes being replaced by other deities (Indra and Prajapati).

The Adityas form a group of solar deities. Their number varied during the Vedic period, but never exceeded twelve. Two supplementary deities were later added to the group made up of Mitra, Varuna (lord and sustainer of the worlds), Aryaman (god of hospitality and the perpetuity of *arya* society), Bhaga (god of the distribution of wealth), Daksha (god of technical ritual skill) and Amsha (god of good fortune), mentioned in the Rig Veda (II, 27, 1). The Brahmanas increased their number from eight to twelve – a number which epic poetry was to take up (see Mahabharata III, 134, 19) – a group of twelve gods sometimes related to the twelve months of the solar calendar.

The eleven Rudras represent a group of gods who were very soon perceived as the multiple manifestations of the god Rudra. Rudra is an ambiguous figure of the pantheon whose sombre face makes him a dangerous being, inspiring the fear of men, but whose shining face at the same time makes him a god who brings good and help, curing all kinds of disease and suffering. He is also given, among others, the antithetical titles of Hara, the 'remover', and Sambhu, the 'one who grants welfare'. This mysterious god, who can spread disease and sow death wherever he goes, is a redoubtable archer, usually living in the heart of the mountains, which is why he is the patron of hunters. While he can ravage cattle, he is above all the one who protects and preserves them, since he is the 'lord of beasts' (*pasupati*). He is also called the divine physician and 'lord of asceticism' (*yogesvara*). These qualities of being protector of domestic animals and the yogin magician already make him the prototype of the god Shiva of classical Hinduism. He is also given the epithet 'benevolent' (*shiva*) in the 'white' Yajur Veda. He may well have originally represented an unpredictable and dangerous divine power. Moreover, it is very probable that several ancient deities, some of which are perhaps not Aryan, were subsequently assimilated to this mysterious force, which was deified in the Vedic period.

The eight Vasus, of which there are several typical lists, represent, or rather embody, certain natural phenomena (fire, water, light, wind . . .). They are presented as the servants of the warlike god Indra.

The *Asvini devatas* or Asvins, also called Nasatya, are twin deities whom Vedic mythology represents

6. Rudra, storm god of the Vedas

under the aspect of two gracious youths crossing the heavens in a gilded chariot with 'three seats, three towers and three wheels' (Rig Veda I, 118), harnessed to flying horses. They are seen at dawn, just before sunrise. With their flask of medicine, filled with honey and cures, they aid and heal both gods (notably Indra) and human beings. They are also invoked at marriages, and at childbirth, to deliver pregnant women. These attributes connect them directly with the third 'function' of Indo-European ideology, that of fertility and production. It is no coincidence that they were the patrons of the 'class' of breeders and farmers (Vaishyas).

The *asuras* (Avestic *ahuras*) are a special class of divine powers common to Indian and Iranian mythologies. In the Indo-Iranian period, the *asuras* (a term derived from *asu*, 'the vital breath') are heavenly deities to whom is attributed a magical and hidden power which the texts call *maya*. In India, this hidden power was to be considered malevolent in the period of the Brahmanas. This interpretation, handed down by a late and erroneous etymology which interpreted *asura* as derived from *a* (privative) and *sura* ('god') = 'non-god' or 'anti-god', ultimately relegated the *asuras* to the status of demons. Furthermore, epic literature opposed the *suras* (the gods) to the *asuras* (the demons). On the other hand, the Iranian world simply kept the idea of the invisible power of the *asuras* and, following the religious reform undertaken by Zarathustra, made the chief or them a superior deity – Ahura Mazda – 'the wise lord', while the *daevas* (the *devas* of the Vedic world) sank to the level of demons, since they were deprived of this occult power. These parallel interpretations ended up denoting contrary realities in Iran and India by the same term (*ahura/asura*).

2. Two sovereign gods, Mitra and Varuna

Several deities of the Vedic pantheon are given the epithet *asura* in the Rig Veda, notably the Adityas, but also Agni, Dyauspita and Rudra. However, it is to Varuna that this title is given in the first place. Very often associated with the god Mitra in the 'pair' Mitra-Varuna, an expression of the complementarity of these two sovereign gods which the Rig Veda does not disown, Varuna appears as one of the most important figures in the Vedic pantheon. He is primarily the sovereign of the worlds 'who has separated the two vast worlds by supporting them, who has pushed up the vast vault of heavens and the stars all at once, and spread out the earth' (Rig Veda VII, 86, 1), 'as a butcher does with a hide, so that it can be a carpet for the sun' (Rig Veda V, 85, 1). This deity is also the guardian of *rta*, cosmic order, moral regularity and ritual norms, since Varuna can distinguish order from disorder (Rig Veda X, 124, 5). Thanks to his magical creative power (*maya*) which allows him to change or create forms, Varuna is the author of the principal natural phenomena: the cycles of night and day, the seasons, the rain. He is also a god who knows and sees everything.

Varuna

Keep fear far away from me, Varuna, and hold fast to me, O emperor of Order. Set me free from anguish as one would free a calf from a rope; I cannot bear to live apart from you even for the blink of an eye.

Varuna the Asura, do not wound us with your weapons that wound the man you seek when he has committed a sin. Let us not be exiled from the light. Loosen clean away from us our failures, so that we may live.

O Varuna born of strength, the homage to you that was made in the past long ago we would speak now, and in the time yet to come. Upon you who cannot be deceived our vows are set, unshakeable, as if upon a mountain.

Abolish the debts for the things I have done, O king, and do not make me pay for what has been done by others. So many more dawns have not yet risen, Varuna; make sure that we will live through them.

If someone I have met, O king, or a friend has spoken of danger to me in a dream to frighten me, or if a thief should waylay us, or a wolf – protect us from that, Varuna.

Do not let me know the loss of a dear, generous, open-handed friend, Varuna, nor let me lack the wealth that makes a good reign, O king. Let us speak great words as men of power in the sacrificial gathering.

(Rig Veda II, 28, 6–11)

Varuna also appears with the features of a formidable god of justice who holds in his bonds the sinner guilty of ritual or moral crimes. He shares his attributes as sovereign god and his cosmic functions, notably that of the guardian of *rta*, with another god, Mitra. Mitra is equally known in the Iranian world where, under the name of Mithra, he is an important solar deity of the Mazdaean pantheon. By contrast, the Indian Mitra does not have a central position in the Veda, and the Rig Veda only devotes a single hymn to him (III, 59). In about twenty Vedic hymns, praises are addressed jointly to the two deities, so that it is sometimes difficult to distinguish what relates to Mitra from what relates to Varuna. It is only in the later Vedic texts, notably in the ritual treatises and the theological commentaries in prose, that Mitra and Varuna are defined in relation to one another.

The etymology of the term *mitra* associates the name of this god with the idea of the 'contract' of which he is in some sense the personification. Mitra helps people to fulfil their commitments while keeping a fair balance between the interests of each of the parties involved. This role of mediator is confirmed by the epithet *yatayajjana*, 'the one who organizes men', an attribute in the hymn which the Rig Veda devotes to him. Seen at a distance from the sombre and violent Varuna, Mitra appears as a god who is close and amiable, and in whom one can have confidence.

In a highly speculative passage in the Satapatha Brahmana (IV, 1, 4), the pair Mitra-Varuna are assimilated to the 'two forces', that is, to the two complementary poles of priesthood and royalty. In this text Mitra represents the archetype of priesthood or spiritual authority (*brahman*), while Varuna represents the archetype of royalty or temporal power (*kshatra*). On a more 'psychological' level, it could be said that Mitra is associated with intention and reflection, while Varuna is bound up with execution, that is, with action. Thus Mitra is the one who knows or conceives; Varuna is the executant, the one who acts. In respect of the Hindu social order, Mitra and Varuna characterize respectively the Brahmins (priests) and the Kshatriyas (kings and warriors), with the idea of the primacy of spiritual authority over temporal power, since the knowledge of which wisdom is the attribute has primacy over action, which is translated by force.

3. A warrior god, Indra

With some two hundred and fifty hymns addressed to him in the Rig Veda, perhaps a quarter of the collection, Indra appears as the most famous and popular god of the Veda. The hymns describe him as a being with marked anthropomorphic features (they mention his arms, his hands, his jaws, his lips, his beard, and so on) and his strong personality (he is an insatiable drinker of *soma* and a lover of gallant adventures), emphasized by the number of adjectives which make him the model 'knight', liberal and generous, and the paragon of the fiery and heroic warrior. Though Indra always performs his warlike exploits as a solitary hero, the Vedic hymns nevertheless give him companions and assistants like the noisy cohort of the storm gods, the young Maruts, sons of Rudra, and the god Vishnu, who traverses space in three leaps, but whose importance in Vedic times seems greater than the texts suggest (only six hymns in the Rig Veda).

The mythology of Indra is centred on warlike themes, notably the Vrtrahatya, 'the killing of Vrtra' (see e.g. Rig Veda I, 32), a heroic battle in which the young hero Indra, armed with his thunderbolt (*vajra*), kills Vrtra, the primordial serpent (*ahi*), who holds in his coils the receptacle containing the original waters and the principles of life. The victorious outcome of this fight over origins described at length in the Rig Veda and in the course of which Indra gets his title of Vrtahan, 'killer of Vrtra', allows the waters to flow. Having become rivers, they can again make the earth fertile for the greatest good of humankind (the *arya*).

The effect of the Vrtrahatya is also to liberate the forces of life, notably light and fire. So this mythological story must first be read as a cosmogonic myth, since the killing of the monster serpent allows an ordered world to come into being (the transition from chaos to cosmos). A hymn (Rig Veda III, 31,15) in fact reports that Indra created the sun, the dawn and fire, while a second passage (Rig Veda VIII, 89, 5) indicates that Indra himself spread out the earth and supported the sky. The liberation of the primordial waters thus allows the appearance of the golden embryo (*hiranya garbha*), the true genetic principle of the primal waters, in the form of a cosmic egg. Its lower shell becomes the earth, its upper part is transformed into the heaven, while at the centre shines the fire which liberates heat and spreads light.

It is also interesting to note that Rig Veda X, 124

Indra

The god who had insight the moment he was born, the first who protected the gods with his power of thought, before whose hot breath the two world-halves tremble at the greatness of his manly powers – he, my people, is Indra.

He who made fast the tottering earth, who made still the quaking mountains, who measured out and extended the expanse of the air, who propped up the sky – he, my people, is Indra.

He who killed the serpent and loosed the seven rivers, who drove out the cows that had been pent up by Vala, who gave birth to fire between two stones, the winner of booty in combat – he, my people, is Indra.

He under whose command are horses and cows and villages and all chariots, who gave birth to the sun and the dawn and led out the waters – he, my people, is Indra.

He who is invoked by both of two armies, enemies locked in combat, on this side and that side, he who is even invoked separately by each of two men standing on the very same chariot – he, my people, is Indra.

He without whom people do not conquer, he whom they call on for help when they are fighting, who became the image of everything, who shakes the unshakeable – he, my people, is Indra.

(Rig Veda II, 12, 1–9)

alludes to the proclamation by Indra of a new cosmic order.

The victory of Indra over Vrtra which sets in motion the flow of waters and the liberation of the principles of life also led this myth to be interpreted in a naturalist sense (the rain let loose by the storm or the triumph of the light [sun] over the cold), so that Indra was regarded as a storm god, all the more so since the *vajra* (missile or thunderbolt) can be interpreted symbolically as the lightning flash which pierces and tears apart the storm clouds, thus unleashing the cataracts of heaven.

Finally, the struggle between Indra and Vrtra can be read in historical terms. Indra would embody the warrior god of the Aryan tribes, helping these latter to conquer new territories during their progress in India. Compared with Indra-Vrtrahan (the 'one who breaks resistance'), Vrtra would represent the 'resistance' of the hostile Dasyus, who have to be conquered for an advance to be made.

4. Two 'liturgical' gods, Agni and Soma

By comparison with Mitra-Varuna, who share the attributes of sovereignty, and the invincible Indra, to whom, it seems, pride of place is given in the Veda, Agni and Soma form a distinct group of very important powers within the Vedic pantheon, that of the sacrificial deities.

Agni 'is' fire (cf. Latin *ignis*) in all its forms. This god has very few anthropomorphic features, but the Vedic hymns which are devoted to him evoke his jaws of gold and flame, his flamboyant hair, his tongue (or seven tongues – one of his epithets is Saptajihva = 'with seven tongues'), which is so strong that it can lick up the offerings of milk or melted butter, which he then takes to the gods. As Agni is present in the three worlds from the origins of the universe, he is sometimes represented as a figure with three heads: in heaven, Agni is the sun; in the atmosphere, he is the lightning-flash which comes from the clouds; and on earth he is both the destructive fire which ravages the forests 'as a buffalo let loose in a flock' (Rig Veda I, 58,4), and

Agni

I pray to Agni, the household priest who is the god of the sacrifice, the one who chants and invokes and brings most treasure.

Agni earned the prayers of the ancient sages, and of those of the present, too; he will bring the gods here.

Through Agni one may win wealth, and growth from day to day, glorious and most abounding in heroic sons.

Agni, the sacrificial ritual that you encompass on all sides – only that one goes to the gods.

Agni, the priest with the sharp sight of a poet, the true and most brilliant, the god will come with the gods.

Whatever good you wish to do for the one who worships you, Agni, through you, O Angiras, that comes true.

To you, Agni, who shine upon darkness, we come day after day, bringing our thoughts and homage,

to you, the king over sacrifices, the shining guardian of the Order, growing in your own house.

Be easy for us to reach, like a father to his son. Abide with us, Agni, for our happiness.

(Rig Veda I, 1)

fire lit by human beings, either for domestic use or for the offering of sacrifices. Agni is an old god, since he is contemporary with the birth of the world, but he is also ever young, since he is rekindled every day: that is why he is called the immortal one, or 'the god who does not age' (Rig Veda I, 58,2).

Agni is equally closely bound up with the element of water. Furthermore, he is called 'bull of the waters', since he makes them fertile (Rig Veda X, 21, 8). Hymn III, 1, 12 calls him 'embryo of the waters', since fire, the male element, penetrates the waters, the female element, the original principle, in order to have offspring by them. Agni is again present in plants, since it is the rubbing together of two pieces of wood which makes fire.

When he denotes more specifically heavenly fire, Agni is given the designation Vaisvanara, 'relating to all men'. He is also called Jatavedas, 'knowing all who are born', since, as the sovereign god, Agni is also bound to the order of the world. Finally, as the privileged witness of family life, he is 'guardian of the hearth', since he protects it. He also follows, stage by stage, the great moments of the lives of all the 'twice born'.

If Agni occupies such an eminent place within the Vedic pantheon, it is because he is the first sacrificer, the 'navel of sacrifices' (Rig Veda VI, 7), and, consequently, the prototype of the priest. This is how he is emphatically celebrated in the first hymn of the Rig Veda.

Thus Agni the offerer is the 'chaplain of man' (Rig Veda III, 3, 2) who serves as mediator between the world of men and that of gods. His role is to make human offerings acceptable to the gods by receiving them in the 'crackling of his flames'; that is why the same hymn also describes him as the 'wondrous messenger who travels between the two worlds'.

Soma is the other of the two liturgical deities. Also known in Iran under the form Haoma, in Vedic India Soma denotes two things which are often difficult to distinguish: on the one hand a heavenly and mythical plant symbolically replaced by various earthly substitutes (hallucigenic mushrooms or plants from the flax family?) and on the other the liquor or divine drink obtained from the stems of this plant, which the officiants prepared and drank at certain solemn sacrifices.

This intoxicating and fortifying drink, which increases sexual energy and stimulates thought, is also an elixir of long life, i.e. etymologically the drink of 'non-death' (*amrta*), ambrosia, the drink of the gods *par excellence*, by which Indra becomes intoxicated before his decisive battle against the demon Vrtra (Rig Veda I, 80, 2). Prepared ritually for sacrifices, the plant soma undergoes numerous treatments before providing this divine nectar

The Preparation of Soma

Butter and milk are milked from the living cloud; the navel of Order, the ambrosia, is born. Together those who bring fine gifts satisfy him; the swollen men piss down the fluid set in motion.

The stalk roared as it united with the wave; for man he swells the skin that attracts the gods. He places in the lap of Aditi the seed by which we win sons and grandsons.

Relentlessly they flow down into the filter of a thousand streams; let them have offspring in the third realm of the world. Four hidden springs pouring forth butter carry down from the sky the ambrosia that is the oblation.

He takes on a white colour when he strains to win; Soma, the generous Asura, knows the whole world. He clings to inspired thought and ritual action as he goes forth; let him hurl down from the sky the cask full of water.

Now he has gone to the white pot coated by cows; the racehorse has reached the winning line and has won a hundred cows for Kaksivat, the man of a hundred winters. Longing for the gods in their heart, they hasten forth.

Clarifying Soma, when you are sated with waters your juice runs through the sieve made of wool. Polished by the poets, Soma who brings supreme ecstasy, be sweet for Indra to drink.

(Rig Veda IX, 74, 4–9)

which gods and officiants will consume together in a shared libation. The ninth book of the Rig Veda, devoted almost in its entirety to the clarification of soma (*soma pavamana*), is a powerful description of this whole process. The stems are washed several times to steep them in water and then they are crushed, either in a mortar by simple pressure (Rig Veda I, 28) or between millstones for a more solemn sacrifice. They produce a precious brown juice which is then poured through a filter of wool or sheepskin to clarify it. The nectar thus obtained is drunk, diluted with milk or water. Consuming it produces a mystical drunkenness and an ecstatic joy which is described particularly well in hymn IX, 119 of the Rig Veda. The soporific drunkenness gives the officiant the impression of now belonging to the divine world, in other words of being immortal.

In the Vedic literature, the successive stages of the preparation of soma are often assimilated to different cosmic or celestial phenomena, because of the 'royalty' of the soma. In fact, if soma is the king of plants and vegetables, it is also the master of visible things and the king of the world. Thus the whole cosmos is contained in power in every pressing of soma: the noise of the turning mills is likened to thunder, the wool filter becomes the clouds, the juice which flows is seen as the sperm provided by the rain that makes the plants grow. That is why Soma is in turn identified with the bull who couples with the cows since, after being pressed, the juice is diluted with milk. Hymn IX, 1 of the Rig Veda says poetically that the 'milk cows suckle their young'. Soma thus becomes the personification of fertile power, of life-giving moisture and more generally of the vital force.

Whatever its real nature and that of the substitutes used by the cult, the plant soma and the intoxication it produces enjoyed a considerable prestige among the Vedic Indians. This is clear from the way in which the Vedic hymns continually celebrate the virtue of this divine drink. The revelation of the possibility of communion between the gods and human beings, and the celebration of the existence of a world of bliss beyond our terrestrial world ceaselessly exalted by the texts were to continue to haunt the whole of Indian spirituality long after the disappearance of the soma sacrifices. The pursuit of the quest of the Absolute necessitated the development of complex psycho-physiological techniques (yogic practices, techniques of mediation and respiration) which Indian thought developed in Vedic times. Some of them have their origin in earlier shamanic and ecstatic practices.

5. Other gods

Indra, Mitra-Varuna, Agni and Soma are the main figures of the Vedic pantheon. Alongside these main deities coexist a multitude of figures of differing importance, and a long series of genies and demons described by a very rich mythology.

Dyauspita, the 'heavenly father', is one of the oldest deities of the pantheon. He is a god who is passive and in retreat, since he was robbed of his prestige at a very early stage by Varuna. His consort, the 'earth mother' Prithivimata, is famed above all for the things that she bears, makes to grow and brings to maturity on her very wide expanses.

These two deities are often invoked together in hymns under the double form Dyavaprithivi.

In the group of solar deities, alongside Surya, the sun as a star, and his aspect as 'vivifier', Savitri (Savitar), who commands the cycle of night and day and therefore rules human activities, we also find the fair and generous goddess Usas, who personifies the dawn and is the most important female figure in the pantheon. The hymns present her in the form of a radiant young woman in a shining dress, or as a desirable woman displaying all her body (Rig Veda I, 123,10). She has the power to turn back the darkness of her sister Night (Nakta), and each morning to awaken everything to life and movement. However, as she renews each day, dawn also takes a day from a person's life.

Vayu is not a simple god of the wind. He is celebrated as a fiery god associated with Indra and as the 'breath' of the world and the universal soul similar to *prana*, the breath of life. In a similar key, Parjanya, the 'giver of rain', personifies the majesty of tropical storms and tempests: he is a noisy god (cf. Rig Veda V, 93), sometimes included among the Adityas.

Originally, Pushan seems to have been connected with the solar myths (cf. Rig Veda VI, 56). Subsequently he became a protector god showing the way to those (men and flocks) who wandered from their ways and protecting them from peril. He

> ## Usas
>
> Like a dancing girl, she puts on bright ornaments; she uncovers her breast as a cow reveals her swollen udder. Creating light for the whole universe, Dawn has opened up the darkness as cows break out from their enclosed pen.
>
> Her brilliant flame has become visible once more; she spreads herself out, driving back the formless black abyss. As one sets up the stake in the sacrifice, anointing and adorning it with coloured ornaments, so the daughter of the sky sets up her many-coloured light.
>
> We have crossed to the farther bank of this darkness; radiant Dawn spreads her webs. Smiling like a lover who wishes to win his way, she shines forth and with her lovely face awakens us to happiness.
>
> Let me obtain great riches of glory and heroic men, Dawn, riches that begin with slaves and culminate in heroes! Fortunate in your beauty, incited by the victory prize, you shine forth with the fame of great achievements.
>
> Gazing out over all creatures, the goddess shines from the distance facing straight towards every eye. Awakening into motion everything that lives, she has found the speech of every inspired poet.
>
> The ancient goddess, born again and again dressed in the same colour, causes the mortal to age and wears away his life-span, as a cunning gambler carries off the stakes.
>
> (Rig Veda I, 92, 4–10)

fashioned the horses of Indra. There is also Visvakarma (literally, he who makes everything), the architect who constructed the universe, and Tvastr, the divine smith who is said to have cast all the metal armour used by Indra against the demon Vrtra.

7. Apsaras (heavenly dancer)

The genies include the seductive Apsaras who live in the water, the air or the forests. These are naiads like the nymphs of Greek mythology. They are most often found linked to another mythological group, the Gandharvas, who are presented as their companions. The Gandharvas are genies of the air and wonder-working powers. The later literature made them divine musicians. The Nagas represent a group of creatures with human faces but midway between dragons and serpents, closely associated with myths about the waters, while the Yakshas, who appear in tree-trunks, are sympathetic and unaggressive genies, like plump dwarfs.

also guides the betrothed going to her future spouse and leads the dead to the other world.

The divine craftsmen also play an essential role in Vedic mythology. By their work and their skill they compete with the action of the gods, since they make their equipment. The triad of the Rbhus (literally 'the skilful ones') comprises Rbhuksan, Vaja and Vibhvan, who are thought to have made the golden chariot of the Nastaya twins and

8. Naga and Nagini (snake deities)

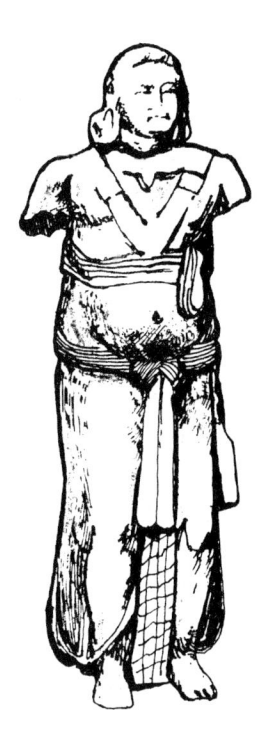

9. Sandstone Yaksha

Furthermore, innumerable demons haunt the stories of Vedic mythology. The most powerful figures are directly linked to the mythology of Indra; mention has already been made of Vrtra, the primal servant, but Indra equally engaged in combat with Arbuda, Pipru, Sambra and Visvarupa, the three-headed son of Tvastr.

Finally, the Rakshashas are malevolent beings, greedy for meat, who seek to disturb the good order of Vedic sacrifices. They are habitually repelled with a request to the god Agni to drive away their evils with the fire of his flame (cf. Atharva Veda VIII, 3). Furthermore, there are several categories of vampires, the Pisachas, demons who eat raw flesh, and the Vetalas, who take possession of dead bodies, which they use as coverings.

Indra slays Vrtra

He slew the dragon and released the waters; he split open the bellies of the mountain. He slew the dragon who lay upon the mountain; Tvastr fashioned the roaring thunderbolt for him. Rejoicing in his virility like a bull, he chose the Soma and drank the extract from the three bowls. Indra killed Vrtra, the greater enemy, the shoulderless one, with his great and deadly thunderbolt. Like the branches of a tree felled by an axe, the dragon lies prostrate upon the ground. For like a non-warrior muddled by intoxication, Vrtra challenged the great hero who had overcome the mighty and who drank Soma to the dregs. Unable to withstand the onslaught of his deadly weapons, he who found Indra an overpowering enemy was shattered, his nose crushed. Without feet or hands he fought against Indra, who struck him upon the back with his thunderbolt. The castrated steer who wished to become the equal of the virile bull, Vrtra lay shattered in many places. Over him, as he lay like a broken reed, the swelling waters flowed for man. Those waters that Vrtra had enclosed with his might – the dragon now lay at their feet.

(Rig Veda I, 32, 3–10)

III
Vedic Beliefs, Speculations and Rites

How did people of Vedic times experience and practise their religion? Before discussing this enormous question, which will involve an analysis of the structures of Vedic 'liturgy' and 'sacrifices', we need to look more closely at the speculative framework in which Vedic cosmology and eschatology are set.

1. Cosmogony

The earliest stories of the birth of the world inserted into certain speculative hymns of the Rig Veda sketch out a variety of cosmogonic scenarios. Three of the main ones are given on the next page.

In Rig Veda X, 129, the universe proceeds from an eternal and undifferentiated (*ekam*) primordial One which comes into being within the mass of primal waters by heating them with its 'creative ardour' (*tapas*) engendered by desire (*kama*) which is at the same time the first seed (*retas*) of consciousness or thought (*manas*): this is the theme of the *hiranya garbha*, the golden embryo, which we met in the mythology of Indra. The link between non-being and being, i.e. the passage from non-existence to existence, is consequently provided by this creative thought which is creative because it desires. Following a process of self-fertilization, the formation of the universe is presented as an engendering. The One seems to bi-polarize itself into male and female forces: in the fifth strophe the text in fact contrasts the 'givers of seed' above and the '(feminine) powers' below. The male powers 'offer' their seed to the female powers, but the latter are free to accept or refuse fertilization.

However, this explanation leaves an enigma, that of the origin of secondary creation and the phenomenal world. Nor does the author of the hymn conceal this. He indicates that it is not the work of the gods, since these came afterwards, with the creation. Only the 'great watcher', regent of the *rta*, Varuna (?), perhaps knows the reply – or perhaps he does not know anything.

According to Satapatha Brahmana XI, 1–6, the hatching of the golden embryo on the surface of the original waters gives birth to the demiurge Prajapati (literally 'the lord of creatures') who, by the sole power of his word, created the three worlds (earth, space, heaven) and the seasons before creating the main deities: Agni, Indra and Soma.

According to Rig Veda X, 90, the universe is the result of the dismemberment by the gods of a primordial cosmic giant, the Purusha, who is 'all that is, was and will be'. The creation appears as the result of the cosmic creative sacrifice of this giant. The particular creations emanate successively from

Three Cosmogonies from the Rig Veda

There was neither non-existence nor existence then; there was neither the realm of space nor the sky which is beyond. What stirred? Where? In whose protection? Was there water, bottomlessly deep?

There was neither death nor immortality then. There was no distinguishing sign of night nor of day. That one breathed, windless, by its own impulse. Other than that there was nothing beyond.

Darkness was hidden by darkness in the beginning; with no distinguishing sign, all this was water. The life force that was covered with emptiness, that one arose through the power of heat.

Desire came upon that one in the beginning; that was the first seed of mind. Poets seeking in their heart with wisdom found the bond of existence in non-existence.

Their cord was extended across. Was there below? Was there above? There were seed-placers; there were powers. There was impulse beneath; there was giving forth above.

Who really knows? Who will here proclaim it? Whence was it produced? Whence is this creation? The gods came afterwards, with the creation of this universe. Who then knows whence it has arisen?

Whence this creation has arisen – perhaps it formed itself, or perhaps it did not – the one who looks down on it, in the highest heaven, only he knows – or perhaps he does not know.

(X, 129)

The Man has a thousand heads, a thousand eyes, a thousand feet. He pervaded the earth on all sides and extended beyond it as far as ten fingers.

It is the Man who is all this, whatever has been and whatever is to be. He is the ruler of immortality, when he grows beyond everything through food.

Such is his greatness, and the Man is yet more than this. All creatures are a quarter of him; three quarters are what is immortal in heaven . . .

When the gods spread the sacrifice with the Man as the offering, spring was the clarified butter, summer the fuel, autumn the oblation . . .

From that sacrifice in which everything was offered, the melted fat was collected, and he made it into those beasts who live in the air, in the forest, and in villages.

From that sacrifice in which everything was offered, the verses and chants were born, the metres were born from it, and from it the formulas were born.

Horses were born from it, and those other animals that have two rows of teeth; cows were born from it, and from it goats and sheep were born . . .

His mouth became the Brahmin; his arms were made into the Warrior; his thighs the people; and from his feet the servants were born . . .

With the sacrifice the gods sacrificed to the sacrifice.

(X, 90)

What was the base, what sort of raw matter was there, and precisely how was it done, when the All-Maker, casting his eye on all, created the earth and revealed the sky in its glory?

With eyes on all sides and mouths on all sides, with arms on all sides and feet on all sides, the One God created the sky and the earth, fanning them with his arms.

What was the wood and what was the tree from which they carved the sky and the earth? You deep thinkers, ask yourselves in your own hearts, what base did he stand on when he set up the worlds?

Those forms of yours that are highest, those that are lowest, and those that are in the middle, O All-Maker, help your friends to recognize them in the oblation. You who follow your own laws, sacrifice your body yourself, making it grow great.

All-Maker, grown great through the oblation, sacrifice the earth and sky yourself.

That which is beyond the sky and beyond this earth, beyond the gods and the Asuras – what was that first embryo that the waters received, where all the gods together saw it?

He was the one whom the waters received as the first embryo, when all the gods came together. On the navel of the Unborn was set the One on whom all creatures rest.

You cannot find him who created these creatures; another has come between you. Those who recite the hymns are glutted with the pleasures of life; they wander about wrapped in mist and stammering nonsense.

(X, 81–82)

the dismembered body of the archetypal Man: what is offered in sacrifices, wild and domestic animals, the strophes (*riks*), melodies (*samans*) and formulae (*yajus*) of the Veda, horses and oxen, the functional classes (*varnas*), the heavenly bodies (moon, sun), the gods Indra, Agni and Vayu, intermediate space, heaven, earth and the four points of the compass. But this sacrifice is a model, since 'with the sacrifice the gods sacrificed to the sacrifice' (Rig Veda X, 90, 156). The Purusha is thus the sacrificial victim, the deity to which the sacrifice is offered and the sacrifice itself.

In Rig Veda X, 81 and 82, the universe is the work of Visvarkarma (literally 'he who does all things'), the universal craftsman, who is in turn divine smith, sculptor and carpenter, and is able to work the many elements. It is thought that here perhaps the term Visvakarma is an epithet meant for another deity (Brihaspati?), who here is celebrated as creative.

In X, 81 we also find the idea of creation sacrifice, since here Visvakarma is simultaneously presented as the one who sacrifices and the victim. However, as in X, 129, it is not clear from what primal matter he drew the visible world. For good measure, the author of hymn X, 82, having taken up the theme of the birth of the One at the heart of the primal waters, adds in conclusion that no one will ever have access to the mystery of origins, since the Wholly Other is like a screen, between human beings and itself.

Visvakarma was later identified with the figure of Tvastr (the 'fashioner'), who is associated with the mythology of Indra. This divine craftsman is the master of forms. He shapes the bodies of certain objects (Indra's weapon) and of animals.

Similarly, the question of the origin of human beings is resolved by several hypotheses. It is said that they are descended from heaven and earth, or again from Prajapati, the original father. Other texts affirm that humanity came forth from the descendants of Yama and his sister Yami (the theme of primitive incest), the progenitors of the first human race. Another mythical figure who is also the first to offer sacrifice, Manu, is sometimes presented as the ancestor of the human race. Like the biblical Noah, this just man is saved from the flood and, after having offered a sacrifice, repopulates the earth (see Satapatha Brahmana I, 8,1).

2. Eschatology

The figure of Yama brings us quite naturally to the great themes of Vedic eschatology. The first ancestor of humankind, Yama (literally the 'twin'), is also the first man to have crossed the gates of the beyond (see Rig Veda X, 14). So he has naturally become the 'lord of the dead' (*pretaraja*) and the 'lord of ancestors' (*pitripati*), who watches over a dark underground world, the entry to which is guarded by two formidable dogs.

Reading the hymns shows us that people of the first Vedic times were more preoccupied with this life than that of the beyond, since they feared death. What they asked above all from the different deities that they invoked was to have a long life and excellent health, and to know a long chain of descendants – in other words, to live a full and happy life, symbolized by the duration of 'one hundred autumns'. While there was no doubt about the existence of another world and the possibility of survival after earthly death, it seems that this was thought of as being very close to earthly life: the one who had died was more or less a double of his earthly being and had the same needs in the beyond as on earth. Furthermore, since there is as yet no question of a soul, strictly speaking – since the notion of *atman* is clearly distinguished only from the Upanishads onwards, it is easy to see how this future life is envisaged in a quite corporeal way.

It has been demonstrated that two eschatological structures with no idea of the judgment of the dead coexist in the Vedic hymns. The first, probably the earliest, represents survival after death as the persistence of the dead person near his tomb or his house, leading a larval and twilight existence in a subterranean abyss like a cave. The second structure, which is more developed because it is later, poses more precisely the question of salvation, or rather of liberation (*moksha*). According to this, the dead person arrives in a paradise by ascending in the smoke from his funeral pyre, with Agni, the god of fire, as his escort. Access to this paradise is essentially determined by the correct observance of funeral rites and the rigorous performance of the appropriate sacrifices. It seems that the interaction of these two structures brought important modifications to the conceptions of Vedic eschatology. The emergence of the notion of paradise tended progressively to obscure everything that no longer evoked a place of heavenly happiness and joy, subsequently provoking a change of orientation in the nature of the subterranean kingdom of Yama. This developed from being a sombre resting place into a place of suffering representing hell (*naraka*).

Furthermore, some texts contrast two ways: a 'way of the gods' (*devayana*) and a 'way of the fathers' (*pitryana*). The first of these two ways links earth to heaven and initially was thought to be taken by the gods when they descended to earth to be present at sacrifices. The second, which links the earth to the subterranean world, was thought to be taken by the spirits of the ancestors, who returned to consume on earth the bowls of rice (*pinda*) prepared for them by their descendants in the rites of *sraddha*, complementary funeral rites intended to transform the dangerous deceased (*preta*) into a benevolent ancestor (*pitr*).

When it was accepted that some individuals attained heaven, the 'way of the fathers' came to be called a 'way upwards', so that other criteria became necessary for distinguishing the 'way of the gods'. The Upanishads touch on this question in affirming that certain 'souls' follow a cycle of rebirths and return to earth: thus little by little the doctrine of transmigration (*samsara*) came to be affirmed. This was finally to form the keystone of all Hindu eschatology.

It seems that contrary to the ancient conceptions of the religions of the hymns, which exalt earthly happiness, people soon came to put more emphasis on the idea of a 'liberation' (*moksha*) in the beyond, while at the same time the speculations on *atman* and *brahman* (see below) intensified and influenced each other. From the first Upanishads onwards, the Self (*atman*) came to be identified with the principle of the energy of the universe and the impersonal Absolute (*brahman*).

In the theological literature of the Brahmanas, the merits accumulated during earthly life, notably by the rigorous offering of sacrifice, do not seem to have had any lasting value, since the people of the Brahmanas feared dying a second time in the beyond, suffering 're-death' (*punarmyrtu*). Since in this ritualistic milieu the only possible refuge was the rite, the Brahmanas advised the construction for oneself in this life, by means of sacrifice, of a new, glorious body which would give the one who sacrificed the same substance as cosmic totality, so that he would thus escape the 're-death' he so feared. On the other hand, the spiritual revolution proclaimed by the Upanishads consisted in affirming, first, that the posthumous destiny of human beings did not depend either on ritual or magical procedures, but only on actions (*karma*); secondly, that the soul or the self (*atman*) is immanent both to the individual and the world; and finally, that only metaphysical intuition (*jnana*) can unveil the true structures of reality. This decisive step, which dissociates the metaphysical knowledge of the facts from the ritual and transforms the material sacrifice into an inner and spiritual sacrifice, led on the one hand to ritual being discredited as ignorant knowledge (*avidya*) that prevented people from being aware of the weight of each of their acts (*karma*), and on the other hand to the identification of ignorance as the first cause of *karma*. The eschatology of the Upanishads thus becomes the belief that those who by metaphysical intuition (*jnana*) have discovered the inner self during this life no longer desire anything and thus no longer 'produce' *karma*; they are eternally freed from time and history and are described as 'delivered beings' (*jivanmuktas*). At their physical death they attain deliverance (*moksha*), while the constituents of their individuality disperse, to return to the nature from which they have been taken. Those who do not yet possess gnosis, do not know; they desire and, by desiring, 'produce' *karma*. At their death they thus follow the cycle of rebirths (*samsara*) in human or animal form, depending on the state of their *karma* at the moment of their physical death.

The Upanishads reinterpret the ancient Vedic distinction between the 'way of the gods' and the 'way of the spirits', which they parallel with ways followed after death respectively by the souls of those who have attained deliverance and the others. According to Brihadaranyaka Upanishad VI, 2, 3, two paths (*srti*) are open to mortals. The first, which is followed by those whom the text calls 'those who know thus' (VI, 2, 15), i.e. the spiritual elite, leads them to the world of the gods (*deva-loka*) and from there towards the sun and the region of brightness, which is why this way is also called the 'solar way'. Having reached that region, a spiritual being (*manasa*) then leads them into the worlds of *brahman*, where they experience eternal happiness. For them there is no return and, according to Kausitaki Upanishad (I, 7) their souls are finally fused in *brahman* after being in communion with it. The second path, that of the spirits, is taken by all those who follow the demands of traditional religion (VI, 2,16), i.e. the practice of sacrifices, alms and mortifications, but who during their existence have not contemplated the divine self. Through the smoke from their pyres, they reach the world of the spirits (*pitr loka*) and the moon, where they become food for the gods. Having completed this step, they regain space and then, by the intermediary of the air and rain, they return to earth, where they become food again. Those who do not know either of these two ways, i.e. those who have lived in ignorance of the sacrifices, 'become worms, insects, all the tribe that bites' (VI, 2, 16). In this case rebirth is automatic and comes about without heavenly retribution or infernal punishment.

3. *Brahman* and *atman*

We have encountered the terms *brahman* and *atman* several times, and without ever having defined them with precision, we have been able to note on the one hand the remarkable range of meaning of the former and on the other the constant semantic development of these two expressions through the different strata of Vedic literature (Samhitas, Brahmanas, Upanishads).

At the end of this general account of the Vedic universe it is necessary to pause a little on these two key notions of Vedic thought and, more broadly, of all Indian religious or philosophical reflection which is inspired by the Veda or claims to derive its legitimation from it.

Regardless of the literary stratum to which they belong, all the texts of ancient Vedism, those of Brahmanism (later Vedism) and also those of classical and modern Hinduism, make innumerable references to the notion of *brahman* (which is a neuter term). The remarkable semantic development of this term prevents us from defining it in a singular formula or translation which would fix it unfailingly in the meaning at a given moment of its history. First, then, let us look at the major stages of its development.

In the Rig Veda, a *brahman* is a 'sacred enigma', a 'mystery' put forward by certain hymns (see Rig Veda I, 152), in other words an enigmatic form of thought which consists of making a correlation, an explicit identification, for example between the rite and the cosmos. This is a literary procedure which the Brahmanas later call *nidana* or *upanishad*. The literary form of this type of language, the *brahmodya* (literally, discourse in the form of *brahman*), which is embodied in the 'enigmatic hymns' of the Rig Veda, then developed through the ritualized dialogue between the main officiants of the cult at the essential moments of the liturgy.

At a second stage, the term *brahman* comes to denote the whole text of the Veda, in other words everything in the Veda which is neither strophe (*rik*) nor melody (*saman*) nor formula (*yajus*), and then the whole of the three collections of the threefold science, the Rig Veda, Sama Veda and Yajur Veda.

For literature of the ritualist type, *brahman* is the fundamental energy which the sacrifice sets in motion and which is to some degree inherent in ritual formula. For the later speculation which will be expressed first in the Upanishads and then in the Vedantic literature, *brahman* becomes the principle of the universe and the root of all phenomenal reality, the transpersonal Absolute, the ultimate basis of all things.

As this substantial base of all things to which everything returns when it disappears, *brahman* then denotes the supreme reality itself; in other words, it is the 'real of the real' (*satyasya satyam*).

Furthermore, *brahman* is not reduced to its function as a substratum of phenomenal reality. It is also consciousness (*cit*) and absolute happiness (*ananda*). This also has an inner dimension which is shown by formulae in the Upanishads of the type *tat tvam asi*, 'You are that'. They form the object of a repeated meditation which transforms the primary meaning of the terms, relating them to each other and dissolving their structures. In this way the 'that' which denotes *brahman* is progressively purified, and stripped of its external appearance and 'third-person' existence. Meditated upon in this perspective, *brahman* appears as both immanent and transcendent, and that is the ultimate justification for its identification with *atman*, the self of the one who meditates on it (see pp. 30f. below).

In this meditation on the interiorization of *brahman*, Sankara (eighth century) and his successors distinguished two levels: a lower level, that of *brahman* 'with attributes' (*saguna brahman*), likened to the supreme lord, creator of the universe and thus existing in a personal mode, and a superior being, *brahman* 'without attributes' (*nirguna brahman*), which is strictly transpersonal. Those who in the course of their life attain the lower *brahman* are on the way to a 'deliverance by stages' (*karmamukti*), while those who succeed in identifying themselves with *nirguna brahman* attain 'immediate deliverance' (*sadyomukti*).

It should be noted, finally, that the term *brahman* (neuter) has several derivatives, notably the masculine noun *brahman* which in later Vedism designates the officiant responsible for silently supervising the sacrifice and ensuring that it is done well, and the neuter noun *brahmana* (literally that which relates to *brahman*), and denotes the vast theological prose commentaries on ritual which forms the second literary stratum of the Vedic texts. This last term, in the masculine, also denotes the whole of the priestly class: the Brahmins.

Unlike the term *brahman*, which has an amazing range of meaning following a long development, *atman*, related to an Indo–European root denoting 'breath' (cf. the German *atmen*), remains more confined within the same network of co-ordinate meanings. The first sense of the term is 'breath', a breath which the Rig Veda connects with the wind: X, 168, 4, which invokes the god Vayu, says that the wind is the 'breath' (*atman*) of the gods. From this initial meaning we then pass to the idea of 'respiration', or 'vital breath' – akin to *prana*, for the vital breath plays the same role in the body as the wind (*vayu*) in the universe – and then finally to the idea of vital principle. The term then denotes what animates, governs and enfolds the constitutive elements of the person, the principle of actions and thought, in short what make a being construct himself and organize himself in such a way as to separate himself from the world around him. In other words, *atman* is what constitutes the self, the supra-subjective individual principle (which is therefore distinct from the function of the self; ego = *ahamkara*) of an individual being, hence the use of this term in Sanskrit as a reflexive pronoun. Furthermore, this term also comes to denote all that is 'one', all that forms a structured totality, and thus the body as opposed to the members, the body as a complete organism. It is apparently from these meanings that the values of distinctive nature, essence and finally soul, which the term *atman* later takes on, derive.

On the basis of a doctrine of correspondences

between the macrocosm (the human being) and the macrocosm (the universe) already known to all ritualist Vedic literature, which was intensified in the Upanishads, Indian speculation came to define an *atman* of the individualized being, an *atman* of the cosmos, the foundation of the universe and universal principle, *brahman*, which at the level of the macrocosm plays the same role as *atman* at the individual level.

According to the conceptions of the Brahmanas, it is by the benefits derived from the practice of sacrifice that the 'soul' prepares itself and 'constructs' itself. By contrast, the literature of the Upanishads affirms that human beings learn to recognize their *atman* in a process of interiorization which make them aware of their real identity. The Taittiriya Upanishad enumerates five 'sheaths' (*koshas*) which cover *atman* and mask its true nature from the 'individual soul' (*jivatman*). When these veils have been lifted by the effect of metaphysical intuition (*jnana*), the being contemplates in himself this divine and eternal self and, grasped by the reality of the Wholly Other, enters into a state of mystical union in which every distinction, all duality between the subject and object, is abolished; then he discovers at the depths of his being that the individual *atman* (*jivatman*) and the *atman* of the universe (*paramatman* = *brahman*) are one and the same reality. That is why, according to Brihadaranyaka Upanishad I, 4, 10, he exclaims *aham brahmasmi*, 'I am *brahman*'. According to the expression in the Upanishads, this crowning of the mystical life constitutes the experience of *advaita* (literally, 'non-duality').

In short, *atman* is the individual's 'self', or the substance of inner unity, which is not dual. This is emphatically confirmed by Mandukya Upanishad V, 2: *ayam atma brahma*, 'this *atman* is *brahman*', in other words, 'This self is b*rahman*'.

4. Vedic ceremonies and rites

Since Vedic civilization did not leave any material traces, and Vedic archaeology is therefore almost non-existent, our knowledge of the earliest Indian religious thought is based on the textual evidence of the Veda. The hymns of the Rig Veda reveal the structure of the pantheon and the major themes of mythology; the Vedic Upanishads bear witness to speculative thought; and finally the liturgical commentaries (Brahmanas) and the Kalpa Sutras, which provide the theological interpretations of ritual and very detailed descriptions of the attitudes and gestures of officiants in the Vedic ceremonies, allow us to understand the morphology and the symbolism of the different rites which characterize Vedism.

The preponderance of practices over beliefs is essential in Vedic India. Vedism is above all a religion of the rite. That is why it has been possible to define Vedism, and to a certain degree Hinduism, as orthopraxy (right action), since strict conformity to the ritual has priority over adherence to dogmas and does not necessarily imply the idea of a personal faith. The notion of faith in the Christian sense in fact has little place in the Vedic world. The Sanskrit term *sraddha* (related to the Latin *credo*), sometimes wrongly translated 'faith', does not denote adherence to a dogma or a theological belief but the trust that one shows in the gods and in the effectiveness of the ritual and the competence of those who perform it. It is also for this reason that in Vedism ritual error was regarded as 'the' major error. Consequently, if we want to understand the Vedic rites in depth we must remember that in India there is no close connection between practices and beliefs; in other words, ritual acts are 'pure acts', which do not depend on intellectual notions. It is also worth noting that for the important mythical episodes, those reflecting cosmic events, there are no equivalent rituals; the interpretations proposed by the literature of the Brahmanas are accounts invented to explain the origin of details in the liturgical ceremony.

The whole Vedic cult is based on sacrifice (*yajna*) performed with absolute power by the priestly class. In the Vedic perspective, sacrifice is primarily a gift which is manifested by oblation (*havis*),

'You are That, Svetaketu'

Uddalaka Aruni said to his son Svetaketu: 'Learn from me the true nature of sleep. When a man sleeps here, then, my dear son, he becomes united with being, he is absorbed into himself, and that is why they say of him that he is sleeping. He is absorbed into himself.

As a bird when tied by a string flies first in every direction, and finding no rest anywhere, settles down at last on the very place where it is fastened, in just the same way, my son, our thoughts, after flying in every direction and finding no rest anywhere, settle down on breath; for indeed, my son, mind is fastened to breath.

Learn from me, my son, what are hunger and thirst. When a man is said to be hungry, water is carrying away what has been eaten by him. Therefore as they speak of a cow-leader, a horse-leader, a man-leader, so they call water which digests food and causes hunger food-leader.

Think of your body, my son, as a growing plant. This plant needs a root. And where could its root be except in food? In the same way, my son, as food too is an offshoot, seek after its root, water. And as water too is an offshoot, seek after its root, fire. And as fire too is an offshoot, seek after its root, Being. All these creatures, my son, have their root in Being, they dwell in Being, they rest in Being.

When a man is said to be thirsty, fire carries away what has been drunk by him. Therefore as they speak of a cow-leader, a horse-leader, a man-leader, so they call fire water-leader.

Think of your body, my son, as a growing plant. This plant needs a root. And where could its root be except in water? In the same way, my son, as water too is an offshoot, seek after its root, fire. And as fire too is an offshoot, seek after its root, Being. All these creatures, my son, have their root in Being, they dwell in Being, they rest in Being.

And how these three beings, fire, water, earth, my son, when they reach man each become threefold, I have already explained to you. Know only that when a man dies his voice passes into his thought, his thought into his breath, his breath into the fire [of the funeral pyre] and the fire into the Supreme Being which is subtle essence.

Now that which is that subtle essence is none other than the self. And you are That, Svetaketu.'

'Father, teach me more,' he asked his father.

'Be it so,' his father replied.

'As the bees, my dear Svetaketu, make honey by collecting the juices of distant plants and reduce the juices into one form, and as these juices have no discrimination, so that they might say, I am the juice of this tree or that, in the same manner, my son, all these creatures, when they have become merged in Being, do not know that they are merged in Being. Whatever these creatures are here, whether a lion or a wolf or a boar or a worm or a midge or a gnat or a mosquito, they are all identical with that Being which is subtle essence.

The whole universe is identical with that subtle essence, which is none other than the self. And you are That, Svetaketu.'

'Father, teach me more,' he asked his father.

'Be it so,' his father replied.

↓

'These rivers, my dear Svetaketu, run, the eastern towards the east, the western towards the west. They go from the ocean and return to the ocean. They become the ocean itself. But once they have become the ocean they are incapable of remembering having been this river or that. In the same manner, my dear son, all these creatures, when they have emerged from Being, do not know that they have emerged from Being. Whatever these creatures are here, whether a lion or a wolf or a boar or a worm or a midge or a gnat or a mosquito, they are all identical with that Being which is subtle essence.

The whole universe is identical with that subtle essence, which is none other than the self. And you are That, Svetaketu.'

'Father, teach me more,' he asked his father.

'Be it so,' his father replied.

'If someone were to strike the root of this large tree here, it would lose sap, but it would continue to live. If one were to strike the trunk, it would lose sap, but continue to live; if one were to strike its branches, they would continue to live. Pervaded by the living Self, that tree stands firm, drinking in its nourishment and rejoicing.

But if the life leaves one of its branches, that branch withers; if it leaves a second, that branch withers; if it leaves a third, that branch withers. If it leaves the whole tree, the whole tree withers.

Understand this, my dear son, when life departs from a man, he dies, but the life which is identical with the subtle essence does not die.

Now that which is that subtle essence is none other than the self. And you are That, Svetaketu.'

'Father, teach me more,' he asked his father.

'Be it so,' his father replied.

'Bring me a fig.' 'Here is one.' 'Break it.' 'I have.' 'What do you see there?' 'Seeds, very tiny.' 'Break one of them.' 'I have.' 'What do you see there?' 'Nothing.'

'My son, the subtle essence is there, and you do not see it. It is by that that the tree stands up, tall though it is.'

'Be confident, my dear son. The whole universe is identified with that subtle essence which is none other than the self. And you are That, Svetaketu.'

'Father, teach me more,' he asked his father.

'Be it so,' his father replied.

'Place this salt in water, and then come to me in the morning.' Svetaketu did as he was asked, and next morning his father said to him: 'Bring me the salt which you placed in the water last night.' The son looked for it, but could not find it because it had dissolved completely. 'Sip the water from the surface,' said the father. 'How is it?' 'It is salt.' 'Sip it from the middle,' said the father. 'How is it?' 'It is salt.' 'Sip it from the bottom,' said the father. 'How is it?' 'It is salt.'

His father explained. 'In the same manner, my dear son, you do not see Being. But it is there. It is this subtle essence. The whole universe is identified with it, and it is none other than the self. And you are That, Svetaketu.'

(Chandogya Upanishad, 6, 8–13)

performed with a view to obtaining prosperity, health or other material advantages from the gods. In this sense, Vedic sacrifice is a technique which makes it possible to appropriate useful powers: it is a *quid pro quo*. Indeed, some Indologists have emphasized that Vedic sacrifices are not thanksgivings but always adjurations. However, the sacrifice is also a consecration since, by virtue of the oblation or the victim sacrificed and by the mediation of the officiant, the person offering the sacrifice (*yajamana*) can pass from the secular world to the sacred world and identify himself with the Absolute: the Satapatha Brahmana (X, 2, 1, 1) affirms that a person is born a second time through sacrifice.

The rites are divided into two distinct groups, each of which has its texts and its prescriptive treatises (*sutras*). 1. Domestic rites (*grihyas*) usually performed by the householder are justified by the tradition based on human memory (*smrti*); these are essentially simple oblations and sacraments marking the strong times of the life of all the 'twice born'. 2. The solemn rites (*srauta*) derive their authority from the non-human revelation of the *sruti* and are practised by a variable number of professional officiating priests because they are so complex to perform. Three types of ritual are distinguished: rituals in which fruit and vegetables or butter are offered, sacrifices requiring the slaughter of animals (deer, horses), and the complex rituals of pressing and offering the plant *soma*.

Presided over by the householder, who is equally responsible for maintaining the domestic hearth (*garhapatya*), the domestic rites primarily comprise all the everyday offerings of cereals (corn, barley and rise) in honour of several deities (Agni, Prajapati, Surya). To these everyday rites are added all the 'great sacrifices' (*mahayajna*), practised each day in the morning and in the evening. There are also seasonal rites linked to the different agricultural festivals, along with particular ceremonies connected with the reception of a guest, the building of a house, moving to a new home. Furthermore, several private ritual ceremonies call on numerous magical practices.

Rites of passage consecrate the major stages of the life of the 'twice-born' from before birth. The function of these rites, called *samskara* (literally 'purification', 'sacrament'), is to purify, to perfect and safeguard a happy transition between two stages of the life of the individual. The texts differ on the number of *samskaras*, but the numbers which keep recurring most often are ten, eleven, thirteen, sixteen, eighteen and sometimes forty. To spare the reader a pedantic listing, here I shall mention only the main ones.

One of the first prenatal *samskaras* is a rite relating to the fertilization and conception of the embryo (*garbha*). This ceremony, called *garbhadhana*, took place at the first menstruation of the young bride, during her fertile period. Practised by the husband, who touched the body of his wife with a special herb, it was accompanied by several oblations and completed with sexual intercourse. During the third month of pregnancy, or sometimes later, the *pumsavana* (*vrata*) (literally [wish for] the procreation of a male) was celebrated; this was meant to ensure the birth of a son. The ceremonies relating to birth (*jatakarma* or *jata-sanskara*) extended over several days and included numerous rites (ablutions, oblations). The father would begin by blowing on the child and whispering in his ear various sacred formulae to strengthen his intelligence; this is the rite of 'engendering intelligence' (*medhajanana*). With a golden spoon, he would give the child a sip of honey and clarified butter. This food, thought to be of a solar nature, had a purifying role. After bathing the child, the father put him on his mother's lap, reciting other sacred formulae, and pronounced wishes for health and longevity. Towards the tenth or twelfth day after birth (the end of the period of impurity), there was the 'giving of the name' (*namakarma*). Between the sixth and ninth months the rite of *annaprasana* marked the weaning of the child and its first taste of solid food; then, between its first and third year came *cudakarana*, the first cutting of the hair. This was done by a professional barber. A similar ceremony for young people (*kesanta*) celebrated the shaving of the first beard around the age of sixteen years (for Brahmins).

Around the age of four of five, children began to learn the alphabet, and young boys gradually approached the most important of all the sacraments, the *upanayana*, which marked their introduction to a teacher and master (*guru*). He taught them the essentials of ritual knowledge which every head of a household had to master. During the course of this initiation, the young boy received from his master's hand the sacred thread which from then on made him a 'twice-born'. The age of *upanayana* varied, depending on the class (*varna*): the sons of Brahmins were initiated at eight, of Kshatriyas at eleven and of Vaishyas at twelve. Having become a *brahmachari* ('one who cultivates *brahman*'), the new initiate, who was committed to remain chaste, left his family to live until the end of his studies in the company of his master.

The end of studies was marked by several rites (*samavartana*). The student asked his master to make him a *snataka* (bathed one). After ritual ablutions which changed his status from celibate student to candidate, he could rejoin his family but had to marry in order in turn to become head of a house. Another sacrament, marriage (*vivaha*), on which we cannot dwell here, transformed him into a real householder.

For young girls, marriage took the place of initiation (Manava Dharma Shastra II, 67). It was the only 'sacrament' for girls celebrated with Vedic mantras. All the other *samskaras* relating to girls had to be practised in silence, as specified by Manava Dharma Shastra II, 66.

The funeral (*antyesti*) was etymologically the 'last offering' (*antya-isti*). It consisted in a whole series of rites to ease the passage of the dead person to the beyond. In general, except for children who had not been initiated and ascetics, the body was buried on a funeral pyre. The *sraddha*, mentioned above, completed the panoply of funeral rites, since it transformed the dead person into a 'father' (*pitr*); in other words, he became a benevolent ancestor.

The Vedic rites of initiation in the life-cycle, retained and sometimes even amplified in Brahmanism and then in later Hinduism, have come down to the present day. The main *samskara* are always celebrated even today, but we need to take account of the many variants linked to specific regions or relative to the caste system.

The solemn rites (*srauta*), all extremely complex, necessitated the presence of specialist officiating priests. The number of these priests depended on the type of sacrifice: just one for the *agnihotra*, the simplest of the solemn sacrifices; sixteen or seventeen for the *soma* ritual. These sacrifices were traditionally offered either in the house or near the abode of the one who wanted them to be performed (the *yajamana*, literally 'he who sacrifices for himself'), generally on ground adjoining the home. At the centre of this the *vedi* (literally 'altar') was made. This consisted in a rectangular excavation covered with armfuls of grass on which the sacrifice was laid. For the most solemn sacrifices, the altar became a brick structure. The Vedic world had no temples and public or collective sacrifices, which is why the solemn sacrifices were also private acts. However, because of the considerable sums needed for these sacrifices, only the richest families could perform them.

The performance of any *srauta* rite called for a long preparation of the sacrificial ground. This preparatory ceremony, called *agnyadhana* or *agnyadheya* (literally, 'installation of the fire'), essentially consisted in the ritual installation of the 'three fires' needed for the sacrifice: laying the fire, lighting the fire by rubbing two pieces of wood together, and keeping the three hearths alight. The fires were arranged on little hearths or clay altars following precise rules. The first sacrificial fire, which was for cooking the offering, was the domestic hearth (*garhapatya*); it was circular and laid west of the *vedi*. The second fire (*ahavaniya*), called 'offertory' and square in form, was made east of the altar. The offerings were put on this fire after being cooked. Finally, to the south, there was the 'south hearth', in a crescent shape. It was to drive away the evil spirits and cook the offerings destined for them. Fire is an essential element in any Vedic sacrifice; it is the vehicle of the offering.

As indicated above, the simplest of the solemn sacrifices was the *agnihotra* (literally 'oblation of fire'). This sacrifice consisted of an offering of milk made every day, in the morning in honour of Surya and Prajapati, and in the evening in honour of Agni and Prajapati, by a priest for the person sacrificing or sometimes by that person himself, provided that he was a 'twice-born'. This sacrifice was sometimes followed by a complementary ritual (*agnyupasthana*), which was both adoration of fire and homage to the cow for giving the milk. Special rites (*darsapurnamasa*) were celebrated at the time of the full moon and the new moon. They consisted in various offerings of rice, clarified butter and cakes, accompanied by a recitation of Vedic texts drawn from the Yajur Veda and the Rig Veda. These rites necessitated the presence of four officiating priests. There were also solemn rites relating to each season.

The *soma* sacrifices seem to have been the most important solemn sacrifices. It has even been said that they characterize Vedic sacrifice. The expression '*soma* sacrifice' covers several complex rituals, of which the sacrificial type is the *agnistoma* (literally the eulogy to Agni), which was celebrated once a year in the spring. Though the pressing of the *soma* was done in a single day, it was preceded by numerous introductory rites which took place over three or four days (purchase of the *soma*, installation of the hearths, mills, sacrificial offerings, and so on). The 'consecration' (*diksa*) of the person offering the sacrifice and his spouse was one of the particularly important preliminary rites. By this ceremony, the person offering the sacrifice, who had also to seclude himself in a hut and fast, prepared himself for the second birth which the sacrifice was to realize in him.

After the *soma* was bought in a ritual purchase, the sacred plant was taken in procession to the place of sacrifice where it was venerated as a king. Then followed several rites, including the *pravargya*, consisting of an oblation of hot milk and butter to the Nasatya twins. The pressing of the *soma* stems only began the day after the consecration of the 'master altar' (*mahavedi*) and the sacrifice of a goat in honour of the gods Agni and Soma. When the installation of the mills and filters was complete, and the ritual goblets (*carnasa*) intended for the main officials and the person sacrificing had been distributed, it was possible to proceed to the first pressing, known as the 'morning pressing' (*pratah savana*). The juice which had been filtered out was used for various oblations. Cakes made of rice and barley flour were also offered. Part of the *soma* was then consumed by the main officiants and the person offering the sacrifice. The noon pressing (*madhyandina savana*) took place in accordance with the same scheme as that of the morning. The principal offering was of sour milk, which had previously been warmed, and it was also at this time of day that the person sacrificing distributed the 'honoraria' (*dakshinas*) to each of the officials. The evening pressing, called the 'third pressing' (*trtiya savana*), was shorter. It included a 'eulogy to Agni' (*agnistoma*) which eventually gave its name to the whole sacrifice. Several more rites followed, notably the sacrifice of a sterile cow and a ceremony of desacralization which allowed the person offering the sacrifice and his wife to regain the profane world without risk. Each of the three pressings was accompanied by many chants and the recitation of hymns.

Other rites came to be added to the *soma* rituals. This was particularly the case with the *vajapeya* (literally 'victory drink'), which entailed a symbolic ascent of the person offering the sacrifice to the sun and a chariot race, and the *rajasuya* (literally 'royal consecration'), which established the legitimacy of a king by an unction (*abhiseka*) sprinkled on his person by the officiating priests and representatives of the people. The rites of the *rajasuya* reactualized the cosmogony, and it was in this way that the newly consecrated king attained a sovereignty extending all over the cosmos.

Certain solemn Vedic sacrifices involved the ritual slaughter of animals (*pasubandha*). The victim (a deer) was attached to the sacrificial stake, and then generally had its throat cut; it was subsequently dismembered and then ritually cut in pieces before being cooked. The epiploon, regarded as the essential part of the victim – 'the juiciest' (Rig Veda III, 21, 5) – was taken out, put on a skewer and then offered to the principal deity (thrown on the fire). This part of the peritoneum was thought particularly precious since it was considered the seat of the victim's *atman*. Part of the animal was then offered as an oblation to several deities, while another, the ritual offering (*ida*), was shared between the officiants and the person sacrificing, and then consumed.

The most solemn bloody sacrifice was the *asvamedha* (literally by 'horse-sacrifice'), celebrated for three days by a victorious sovereign. At it, a horse and several other animals were solemnly sacrificed. This sacrifice also involved rites with *soma*. The extremely long preparation for this ritual necessitated a year of preliminary rites. The rites following the sacrifice proper were often just as long.

PART TWO

From Vedism to Hinduism

I
The New Literary Sources

It is customary to distinguish an intermediate phase between ancient Vedism and the classical Hinduism which emerged from the Hindu synthesis achieved round about the Christian era (between the third and fifth centuries); this is called Hinduizing Brahmanism. It is quite difficult to give a precise date to this phase, but it is at all events contemporary with the great religious reforms of the sixth century BCE which resulted in the birth of Buddhism and Jainism. Furthermore, its appearance coincides in time with the end of the activity of Vedic ritual. It corresponds to the centuries during which new concepts were set in place which gave rise to the 'birth' of Hinduism. In fact it began at the end of the period of the Brahmanas, in two types of texts, the Aranyakas and the Vedic Upanishads. This phase is characterized by certain speculative advances, in particular by the generalization of the notion of *brahman* conceived as the trans-personal Absolute, and proclamation of an identity in nature between *brahman* and *atman*. Furthermore, in some Upanishads we find the notion of *bhakti*, 'devotion', shown to a deity conceived of as supreme, or to a guru, and the replacement of the way of acts (*karma marga*) with the way of knowledge (*jnana marga*). This inevitably led to the devaluation of the Vedic sacrifice in favour or a totally inward allegorical sacrifice and of course resulted in a weakening of the ancient pantheon. In substance, the revolutionary message that the Upanishads brought to the Vedic world was that 'the Absolute is not to be done; it is'.

However, this transitional phase should not give us any illusions. It is simply a convenient point of reference indicating that from the Brahmanas to the Vedic and then the post-Vedic Upanishads there is a progression, in stages, from an ancient Brahmanism, that of the Vedic hymns and sacrifices, to a later form, in part developing tendencies contained in nucleus in the Veda. Consequently there is no question of a break with ancient Vedism, and it is better to regard Hinduism as a single whole, without attaching too much importance to superficial divisions. Indeed, it is best to see Vedism as the earliest form of Hinduism and to be careful not to neglect its witness; otherwise everything that came after would be inexplicable.

Centred on costly and complex sacrificial rituals, almost always requiring the presence of several officiating priests, over the course of centuries Vedic religion became the prerogative of a close caste of priests who were jealous of their privileges and transmitted from father to son the prerogatives of a lucrative priesthood. At the same time, and perhaps in reaction to the power of the Brahmins, other religious categories emphasized their difference: the anchorites and itinerant ascetics. Having stripped themselves of everything, they penetrated the solitude of the forests where, living on alms, they practised asceticism (*tapas*) and penitence with faith. Several Vedic Upanishads come from this ascetic milieu or at least reflect its ideas. That is the case with the Mundaka Upanishad. While accepting the value of ritualism (I, 2, 10), this Upanishad specifies very clearly (I, 2, 10) that ritual acts are not always sufficient to ensure definitive liberation, which is without return or rebirths.

In fact, offerings and sacrifices provide only transitory merits. When these are exhausted, one falls back 'into this world or into an even lower world' (I, 2, 10). The Mundaka Upanishad makes a stinging disclaimer of the Brahmanic view that it is possible to accumulate paradises by means of pious liturgical acts: 'The *brahman* who thinks that worlds are constructed by action should despair: the uncreated cannot come forth from the created' (I, 2, 12). If the Brahmin wants to know this uncreated, he must make himself the disciple of a qualified master who will teach him. To sum up, to be totally freed from the cycle of rebirths, a person must accede to the knowledge of *brahman* by the knowledge which alone can take him beyond the cycle of *samsara*.

Some scholars have also claimed that during this period the class of warriors (Kshatriyas) had been able to play a role in the Hindu religious scene and perhaps had supported certain circles in which the Upanishads were developed. While there is no evidence of this, it is nevertheless the case that a number of Upanishads retain the memory of several kings who were profoundly versed in religious questions. We see them organizing theological jousts with famous Brahminic masters, for whom they often provided brilliant competition. The speculations developed in the Upanishads are not the privilege either of the Brahmins or of a particular caste. If this knowledge, though secret, could be given to any individual from the moment that he was qualified to understand it, it was also because a large part of the knowledge in question was not religious but was general information about the material and human universe.

Furthermore, the reaction of the indigenous traditions when confronted with the progress of the 'Aryan' conquest also contributed to the fall of Vedic Brahmanism. In fact, the further the 'Aryans' progressed into the plain of the Ganges, the less they were able to prevent Vedic culture from

---

The Self and Immortality

He knows that highest home of Brahman, in which all is contained and shines brightly. The wise who, without desiring happiness, worship that, transcend this seed, they are not born again.

He who forms desires in his mind, is born again through his desires here and there. But to him whose desires are fulfilled and who is conscious of the true Self, all desires vanish, even here on earth.

That Self cannot be gained by the Veda, nor by understanding, nor by much learning. He whom the Self chooses, by him the Self can be gained. The Self chooses him as its own.

Nor is that Self to be gained by one who is destitute of strength, or without earnestness, or without right meditation. But if a wise man strives after it by those means, then his Self enters the home of Brahman.

When they have reached the Self, the sages become satisfied through knowledge, they are conscious of their Self, their passions have passed away, and they are tranquil . . .

As the flowing rivers disappear in the sea, losing their name and their form, thus a wise man, freed from name and form, goes to the divine which is greater than the great.

He who knows that highest Brahman becomes Brahman. In his race no one is born ignorant of Brahman. He overcomes grief, he overcomes evil; free from the fetters of the heart, he becomes immortal.

(Mundaka Upanishad III, 2, 1–9)

becoming mixed with the indigenous traditions. The external pressure of the indigenous religious cultures, combined with an internal evolution, forced Vedism to take up a certain number of popular beliefs and un-Aryan religious traditions, and then to integrate them. It is difficult today to assess this indigenous contribution to Hindu religion, since it has been largely transformed by Brahminic culture. However, it is certain that the rapid promotion of the gods Vishnu and Shiva, who are known from the Vedic period but did not have a central place at that time, is a result of this fusion between the Vedic sources and some traditions of pre-Aryan cultures.

After the sixth century BCE, ancient Vedism and its ritual died. Nevertheless the Veda remains the point of reference in religious matters, though other texts make an appearance. The pantheon is transformed: important Vedic deities lose their prestige while others who are less celebrated in the hymns undergo an exceptional promotion. Vedic Brahmanism becomes blurred, giving way to other religious forms, but the links with Vedic times remain real. The transition from Hinduizing Brahmanism is to some degree confirmed by the development of the term *brahman* which, down to the modern period, continued to be the pivot around which the whole of the religious and philosophical speculation of Hinduism was organized.

The religious literature of post-Vedic Brahmanism prepared for Hinduism. Again written in Sanskrit, in essentials it comprises three types of texts, the composition of which extends from the end of Vedic times (around the fifth century BCE) to the first millennium of our era. First comes literature of a Vedic kind constituted by the imposing literary mass of the post-Vedic Upanishads (of which there are more than two hundred) and by all the legal treaties (Dharma Shastras), which codify the religious and moral behaviour of individuals in society. Epic literature, centred on two voluminous poems, the Mahabharata and the Ramayana, sometimes compared to the two Homeric epics, represents a second type of text. A third category of works is made up of the Puranas, which are not always distinct from the epic genre, and a considerable group of texts known under the generic name of Tantras. The Puranas are treatises about cosmogony (the birth and dissolution of the universe), mythology (divine genealogies), the history of human civilizations and a quantity of myths and legends. The Tantras, revealed by particular deities perceived as major within the 'sects' (*sampradaya*), form a voluminous esoteric literature of which several types have been listed, corresponding to the major religious families of Hinduism (Vishnuism, Shivaism, Shaktism).

To the literary sources of Hinduism are to be added philosophical literature which emerged from the six Brahmanic *darshanas* (literally 'perspectives [on the real]') and a vast non-Sanskrit religious literature written either in neo-Indian (Bengali, Hindi, Maratha) or Dravidian languages (Kannada, Tamil, Telugu).

1. The post-Vedic Upanishads and the Dharma Shastras

The fourteen Vedic Upanishads, of which a summary table is given on p.10, are the earliest documents of this literary genre, though they are only a very small part of it. Though their chronology is difficult to establish, their composition seems to extend roughly between the sixth and third centuries BCE, the earliest being the Brihadaranyaka Upanishad and the Chandogya Upanishad.

In a late group of Vedic Upanishads which includes the Svetasvatara Upanishad, it has been thought possible to discern the transition from Vedism to Hinduism (Brahmanism). In fact this Upanishad, in which several currents from different eras cross, brings certain significant innovations. It gives a quite special place to a new notion, that of the threefold *brahman*, and, marked by the theistic current, goes on to postulate the idea of a supreme god who in Vedic is called supreme self (*mahatman*). This supreme god who 'in this world makes the wheel of *brahman* turn' (VI, 10, i.e. the cosmic wheel which symbolizes the evolution of life), is defined as the god Rudra Shiva, who can be known by devotion (*bhakti*). Furthermore, the Upanishad also emphasizes (VI, 23) a notion which was to have a great future in the Hinduism of the 'sects', that of the spiritual master (*guru*). From now on knowledge (*jnana*) is no longer enough for *atman* to realize its fusion with *brahman*; it must also benefit from the 'grace' (*prasada*) of the deity. Within rising Hinduism, this Upanishad is already preparing a new way of salvation, the 'way of devotion' (*bhakti-marga*), a way of devotional fervour or, rather, of the 'abandonment of love', which is the basis of Hindu cults.

Furthermore, the Svetasvatara Upanishad (VI, 1, 3) indicates that *samkhya* and *yoga* can serve as ways of access to this Absolute (here Shiva). It is one of the very first documents to give information on these disciplines.

The number of post-Vedic Upanishads cannot be fixed precisely, but it is over two hundred. Their redaction extends over an extremely long period: the first Upanishads go back to the end of the Vedic period and then they extend regularly across the centuries to the modern era. Mention might be made of the Allah Upanishad dating from the sixteenth century, and characteristic of the Hindu–Muslim syncretism of the period. In it, Mitra-Varuna, Allah and the Prophet Muhammad are invoked together. For the contemporary period there is the Ramakrishna Upanishad, which bears the name of a great saint of the nineteenth century, Paramahamsa Ramakrishna (1836–1886). If, as scholars suggest, the Ulladu Narpadu (literally 'Knowledge of Being'), composed in Tamil by Ramana Maharshi, is regarded as an Upanishad, it is certainly one of the most contemporary, since in forty verses it expounds the teaching of its author, who died in 1950.

The post-Vedic Upanishads are usually grouped by genre. A distinction is generally made between the Samanyavedanta Upanishads (literally the Upanishads of the common Vedanta), which pursue teaching along the lines of the Vedic Upanishads; the Yoga Upanishads, which discuss methods of realization by yoga; the Samnyasa Upanishads (literally, 'Upanishads of renunciation') centred on the figure of the one renouncing, which present the point of view of the ascetics (*samnyasin*); and the so-called 'sectarian' Upanishads (Vishnuite, Shivite and Shakta) which belong to the great religious families of Hinduism.

The Muktika Upanishad (I, 1, 30–39) gives a traditional list of 108 important Upanishads. This list comprises twelve Vedic Upanishads and ninety-six post-Vedic Upanishads which are divided as follows: twenty-three Samanyavedanta Upanishads, twenty Yoga Upanishads, seventeen Samnyasa Upanishads, fourteen Vishnuite Upanishads, fourteen Shivaite Upanishads and eight relating to the Shakta cult.

The notion of *dharma* (literally 'law', 'norm', 'order') is one of the basic concepts of Indian thought. This term in part overlaps with the Vedic notion of *rta*, the order of things in ancient Brahmanism, which we encountered in the Vedic mythology of the sovereign gods Mitra and Varuna. However, while *rta* (literally agency) is in practice understood only on the cosmic and ritual levels, *dharma* has more of an essential moral dimension. It is difficult to give a satisfactory translation of the term, since no translation can present the whole of the concept. To simplify, it could be said that *dharma* is of the social and cosmic order, which competes for the balance, maintenance and conservation of the 'triad of worlds' (*triloka*): heaven, intermediary space and earth (and also heaven, earth and the underworld). In keeping with this universal natural law which rules and supports the universe, each element of the macrocosm – and thus also the human being – has a specific *dharma* which could be defined as being in constant conformity with its intimate essential nature. Each element of the universe, by conforming to its own nature, thus makes its personal contribution to the general order of the world. On the other hand, behaviour which runs counter to *dharma* exposes the person who engages in it to serious problems. If society neglects the prescriptions of *dharma* or if the members of the different *varnas* neglect their 'proper duty' (*svadharma*), the whole world will be in danger of collapsing. Every abnormal event that happens indicates that the order of things has been disturbed. That is why the idea finally became established that it was better to act in a mediocre way in accordance with one's own *dharma* than to perform that of another correctly (cf. Bhagavad Gita III, 35; XVIII, 47).

The prescriptions relating to *dharma* are brought together in a vast literature which mixes up civil and criminal matters, religious law, rules of ethics and customs. The Dharma Shastras (literally 'teachings on the law') collect together all the rules which codify human behaviour within the regime of functional castes (*varnas*), and each of the four stages (*ashramas*) of ideal Indian life. This group of texts, which comprises more than seven thousand manuscripts, is itself the direct heir of the Vedic Dharma Sutras (literally 'aphorisms on *dharma*'). But if the latter were still very preoccupied with prescriptions of a ritual or religious kind, the Dharma Shastras put more emphasis on a social or individual morality and on secular law.

The Manava Dharmashastra (literally 'teaching on the law of Manu'), better known in the West under the title Laws of Manu, is certainly the most famous of the Dharma Shastras. This treatise, divided into twelve sections (*adhyayas*), opens with a cosmogonic poem in which Manu, the legislator of the present cycle of humanity, retraces the birth of the world (I, 5–79) and then expounds the theory of the ages of the world (I, 80–87), followed by reflections on the caste system. The eleven other sections of the book deal with rites of passage (*samskara*), marriage and the duties of the householder, the duties of ascetics, the conduct of kings, civil and criminal justice, the question of mixed castes, expiations and *samsara*.

2. The epic literature: the Mahabharata and the Ramayana

Epic Indian literature originates from certain texts of the Vedic era like the dialogue hymns in ballad form in the Rig Veda or the narrative texts in prose included in certain parts of the Brahmanas, which were recited at certain solemn sacrifices like that of the horse (*asvamedha*). To this basis were added yet other texts, in particular all the legends (*itihasas*) and stories which were told by the court poets (*sutas*) and the guilds of itinerant bards (*kusilavas*), a whole ancient literature, often with mythological cosmogonic or legendary themes, which certain Upanishads went so far as likening to a 'fifth Veda' (cf. Chandogya Upanishad VII, 1, 2, etc.).

It is from this material of the Vedic or post-Vedic period that the two epics, the Mahabharata and the Ramayana, were developed, probably between the fourth century BCE and the fourth century CE. So many generations of authors have contributed to shaping these texts that we cannot say much about their authorship. However, the first of the two poems is attributed to the legendary Vyasa, the compiler of the Veda (Vedavyasa); the second is attributed to Valmiki, whose historical reality has disappeared behind the veil of legend.

Attached to the literary cycle of the sacred texts of memorized human tradition (*smrti*), this epic literature helped to promote new divine figures. Its appearance marks the entry of Hinduism on the Indian scene in force.

The pearl of Indian Sanskrit literature, the Mahabharata (literally 'the great [story of the war] of the Bharata'), is also one of the longest poems in world literature. This text, comprising more than 90,000 verses (*slokas*), is divided into eighteen books (literally *parva*, 'articulation'). To these must be added some later passages in prose. It also has a 'supplement' (*khila*), the Harivansa ('genealogy of Hari' = Vishnu), an epic poem in three sections, containing myths, legends and hymns to the glory of the god Vishnu.

The central theme of the Mahabharata is organized around the struggle for sovereignty over the city of Hastinapura, waged by two lines of the descendants of Bharata. On one side are the hundred sons of the blind king Dhritarastra, the Kauravas, and on the other side their cousins, the five sons of Pandu, the Pandavas (Yudhisthira, Bhima, Arjuna and the twins Nakula and Sahadeva), led by the oldest of them, Yudhisthira.

Interpretations of the origin of this vast poem differ. Some scholars have suggested that it is the elaboration of a distant historical event. However, others believe that the Mahabharata depends closely on very ancient mythical or theological structures. The tremendous conflagration at the heart of the Mahabharata, in which the majority of the combatants perish, serves to relieve the earth of a surplus population which it can no longer tolerate, while the figures in the book are supernatural beings incarnated by Brahma. Thus it can be argued that the Mahabharata is the transposition into the human world of a vast system of mythical representations. The poem is essentially the translation of a myth about a great global crisis into human terms: the confrontation of the forces of good and evil develops into a destructive paroxysm which ends up with a rebirth.

Integrated into the Mahabharata, of which it now forms chapters 25 to 42 of Book VI (*Bishmaparvan*), the Bhagavad Gita (literally 'The Song of the Divine One') is an independent literary complex, the form of which in many respects recalls the style of the Upanishads. It is by far the most famous book in all Indian literature. This text, in seven hundred *slokas* divided into eighteen songs, which critics place in the second or first century BCE, reports in dialogue form the long conversation between the third Pandava, the archer Arjuna, distressed at having to fight against his own cousins, and Krishna, his charioteer, just as battle is being joined on the Kurukshetra in the plain near to the city of Hastinapura (now north-east of Delhi).

When conches, horns and drums announce the beginning of hostilities with a deafening noise,

> ## Disinterested Action
>
> *Krishna:*
>
> Set your heart upon your work, and never on its reward. Do not work for a reward, but never cease to do your work.
>
> Do your work in the peace of Yoga and, free from selfish desires, do not be moved in success or in failure. Yoga is evenness of mind – a peace that is ever the same.
>
> Work done for a reward is much lower than work done in the Yoga of wisdom. Seek salvation in the wisdom of reason. How poor those who work for a reward!
>
> In this wisdom a man goes beyond what is well done and what is not well done. So go to wisdom; Yoga is wisdom in work.
>
> Seers in union with wisdom forsake the rewards of their work, and free from the bonds of birth they go to the abode of salvation.
>
> (Bhagavad Gita II, 47–51)

Arjuna weakens (I, 28–31), since he cannot resolve to fight against his relations. He does not aspire either to victory or to earthly sovereignty. Why, he thinks, gain earthly sovereignty if one's soul is for ever stained with the sin of having massacred one's family? How can he have any delight in this victory? Only evil can come of it, bringing the ruin of the whole family and its sacred traditions. 'On hearing this, Arjuna dropped his bow and arrows and sat on the floor of his chariot in despair' (I, 47).

Krishna, his charioteer, urgently exhorts him to dispel thought unworthy of a member of the class of the Kshatriyas, whose *dharma* is essentially to fight (II, 31). The warrior who refuse to fight, Krishna tells him, renounces his duty and is guilty of sin and dishonour (II, 33). No one can refrain from action: the one important thing is the act (to do one's duty), not the fruits of this action. Krishna teaches Arjuna that it is necessary to consider only the act which is performed, without any desire or any attachment.

> # The Attainment of Deliverance
>
> *Krishna:*
>
> Those who set their hearts on me and ever in love worship me, and who have unshakable faith, them I hold to be the best Yogis.
>
> But those who worship the Imperishable, the Infinite, the Transcendent unmanifested; the Omnipresent, the Beyond all thought, the Immutable, the Never-changing, the Ever One;
>
> Who have all the powers of their soul in harmony, and the same loving mind for all; who find joy in the good of all beings – they reach in truth my very self.
>
> Yet greater is the toil of those whose minds are set on the Transcendent, for the path of the Transcendent is hard for mortals to attain.
>
> But they for whom I am the End supreme, who surrender all their works to me, and who with pure love meditate on me and adore me – these I very soon deliver from the ocean of death and life-in-death, because they have set their heart on me.
>
> Set your heart on me alone, and give me your understanding: in truth you shall live in me hereafter.
>
> (Bhagavad Gita XII, 2–8)

> # In Praise of Krishna
>
> *Arjuna:*
>
> How could they not bow down in love and adoration before you, God of gods, Spirit Supreme? You creator of Brahma, the god of creation, infinite, eternal, refuge of the world! You are all that is, and all that is not, and all that is Beyond.
>
> You are God from the beginning, God in man since man was. You are Treasure supreme of this vast universe, the One to be known and the Knower, the final resting place. You are the infinite Presence in whom all things are.
>
> You are Vayu, Yama, Agni, Varuna, the god Luna, Prajapati and Brahma, the ancestor of all. A thousand homages to you, and again and again, homage to you!
>
> In a vision I have seen what no man has seen before: I rejoice in exultation, and yet my heart trembles with fear. Have mercy upon me, Lord of gods, Refuge of the whole universe: show me again your own human form.
>
> I yearn to see you again with your crown and sceptre and circle. Show yourself to me again in your own four-armed form, you with infinite arms, infinite form.
>
> (Bhagavad Gita XI, 37–46)

This detachment from the result of actions is an excellent introduction to methods (*yoga*) which make the attainment of deliverance (*moksha*) possible. The term *yoga*, which in this context denotes more of a 'unitive discipline' unifying sense and thought in its purest form, that of *bhakti yoga*, gives the *bhakta* (the faithful on the way of the 'abandonment of love') the possibility of recognizing Vishnu-Krishna as the universal Lord (*bhagavan*) by abandoning himself totally to him. The way of *bhakti*, a way of total abandonment to the 'Lord', allows the faithful to benefit from divine grace (*prasada*), to communicate fully with the divine person of his chosen deity (*ishta devata*) and to attain deliverance (*moksha*).

In hymn XI, which is the climax of the Gita, at the request of Arjuna, who asks his charioteer to reveal his universal and sovereign form to him (XI, 3), Krishna, in a particularly eloquent theophany, reveals himself as being himself this lord of the universe, 'manifested' in the human form of the *avatar* (literally 'descent') of Krishna, who has come to save all those who seek him with faith and sincerity. In a vision, Krishna confers divine grace on Arjuna, who can then contemplate the multiple forms and manifestations 'by the hundreds and

The Mahabharata

So vast is the Mahabharata that it is not easy to illustrate; so vast indeed is it that complete translations run into many volumes (from seven to eleven). Because of its length, many popular versions have been made, often with illustrations. Even they can run to many hundred pages. To give some indication of why the Mahabharata exercises such attraction, here is just one episode in a modern retelling, Arjuna's victory over Radheya, the two most famous archers in the world in single combat.

Raheya sent a powerful arrow to kill Arjuna. The impact was just terrible. It fell on Arjuna's chest and he fainted. The Pandavas thought that he was dead. It was a great moment for the Kauravas. They were sure Arjuna was killed. But before they could cheer Arjuna recovered from the faint. His eyes took on a crimson hue. He felled the banner of Radheya. The glittering banner fell on the ground looking like a fallen rainbow. With the fall of that banner fell all that was dear to Raheya: his fame, his name. The heart of the Kauravas broke when they saw the proud banner of Raheya lying on the ground, drenched in the blood of Raheya. He tried once again to lift up his chariot. He could not. He gave up all hopes now. But still he was trying. He was on the ground with his two arms straining at the wheel. His veins were like whipcords. His face was wet with sweat and blood pouring down his temples. His eyes were raining tears of mortification.

Krishna said: 'Arjuna, you must hurry. You must kill Radheya before he comes back to the chariot.' Arjuna took up an arrow which was like a thunderbolt. Looking at it, the Kauravas lost heart. Arjuna invoked the divine astra and fixing the arrow to his bow he pulled the string to his ears. He released the arrow. The sky was illuminated by the splendid arrow as it sped on its way. Raheya was bending down: his arms were still trying in vain to lift up the chariot. The arrow of Arjuna came very near him. Raheya just looked at it and, even as he was looking at it with a smile of sheer contempt in his eyes, it cut the head of the great Raheya. The head of the great commander of the Kaurava army fell on the ground like the sun suddenly descending to the earth. His handsome face still bore the smile and his lower lip was caught between his teeth in his efforts to raise the chariot. A glow left the body of Raheya and went upwards to the sky. There were some who could see this. The glow went slowly, so slowly that it looked as though it were unwilling to leave that beautiful body which had held it for so many years.

(version by Kamala Subramaniam, Bharatiya Vidya Bhavan, Bombay 1965)

---

thousands' of Krishna, which so far have been revealed to no one (XI, 6). Thus Arjuna sees all the deities of the Veda passing before him: Aditya, Vasu, Rudra, Asvin, Marut (XI, 6). Seized with fear and wonder at this vision, he exclaims in wonder.

In hymn XII, Krishna expounds his doctrine of *bhakti yoga*, the 'discipline of devotion', the third mode of liberation alongside liberation by action (*karma yoga*) and liberation by knowledge (*jnana yoga*). Those who absorb their spirit in him, i.e. those who devote themselves to *bhakti yoga*, are the most accomplished yogis. However, Krishna affirms that those who honour 'the imperishable which cannot be defined or manifested' (the adepts of *jnana yoga*) also find their way to him. These are not wrong in their aim, but the way which they follow is much more difficult because it is more mortifying. Verse 5 in fact indicates that it is far more difficult to attach oneself to the 'non-manifest' (the trans-personal Absolute) than to the 'manifest' (the personal absolute). According to the Gita, it is not because the difficulty of this way is greater that it is higher or more efficacious. The 'easier' way preached by Krishna leads more naturally to the same goal.

Hymns XIII to XVIII expound teaching on the theory of knowledge and on the interplay of the three attributes (*gunas*) of fundamental nature (*prartri*). Hymn XVIII, which ends the poem, also develops a doctrine of liberating renunciation in which the abandonment of the fruit of action (*tyaga*) is presented as having a wider scope than renunciation (*samnyasa*).

Then, at the end of the last chant, Arjuna, cured of his doubts by the teaching of Krishna, declares that he is again ready to fight: 'My confusion is dispersed; thanks to you . . . I have recovered my presence of mind. Here I stand, freed from doubt. I will execute your command' (XVIII, 73). The war of the Bharatas can then begin. The end of the sixth book of the Mahabharata is devoted to a detailed description of the first ten days of this war.

It has been said that the Bhagavad Gita played the role of a kind of 'gospel' of Hinduism in India. Such, in fact, has been its renown that unlike the rest of the Mahabharata, which is incorporated into the literary cycle of the *smrti* (human memory), the Song of the Divine One is part of the cycle of divine revelation (*sruti*). It has profoundly marked the spirit of people and has been the object of an important series of commentaries all down the ages, from that of Sankara (788–820) to the contemporary commentaries of B. G. Tilak (1856–1920), Aurobindo Ghose (1872–1950) and A. C. Bhaktivedanta Swami Prabhupada (1896–1977).

In the Gita, Krishna announces a new way of deliverance, addressing the average person who, while living in the world, also seeks to be saved. In contrast to the ascetics who refuse to act, the Bhagavad Gita, without being an apologia for action, teaches that everyone must conform to his 'own *dharma*' (*svadharma*), act by duty, but detach himself from the fruit of his acts. The personal effort furnished by the *bhakta* promotes in him the reception of divine grace which allows him to accede to the knowledge of God. So if the Gita has enjoyed great success over more than twenty centuries, it is because it reduces the incompatibility between the demands of normal practical life and strict asceticism.

The second epic, the Ramayana (literally the acts of Rama), which is shorter than the Mahabharata – 24,000 *slokas* divided into 7 sections (*kandas*) – recounts the story and adventures of the divine hero Rama, one of the four sons of Dasaratha, king of the city of Ayodhya. Rama and his wife Sita, the adopted daughter of Janaka, a king of Videha, are the very model of conjugal fidelity. Having grown old, Dasaratha wants Rama to succeed him on the throne. But as the result of a machination, Kaikeyi, one of the wives of Dasaratha, to whom he had promised to grant a wish one day when she had helped him as he was wounded, persuades the king to exile Rama and install on the throne her own son, Rama's half-brother. After his son has left for exile, Dasaratha dies of chagrin and despair. In the forest of Dandaka, where Rama has taken refuge with his wife and another of his half-brothers, Lakshmana, he has to engage in several combats with the Rakshasas, the demons. However, their chief, Ravana, by means of a trick, succeeds in kidnapping the beautiful Sita and carrying her off to his capital of Lanka (Ceylon?). Rama and Lakshmana go in search of Sita and are informed by a monster named Kabandha that Rama could regain his wife if he allied himself with the king of the monkeys. Rama and Lakshmana then meet the king of the monkeys, Sugriva, and help him to reconquer the kingdom that his brother Balin had stolen from him. Then, thanks to Hanuman, head of the army of the monkeys, Sita is rediscovered on the island of Lanka. There follows a gigantic battle in which Rama and his allies face the Rakshasas; in the course of this battle the chief of the demons is killed by Rama. Rama rediscovers Sita, but immediately repudiates her, thinking that he cannot keep as his spouse a woman who has lived with another. Sita then asks for divine judgment. A pyre is built on which she is to be burnt alive, but Agni, the god of fire, withholds his body. After this proof indicating the unfailing fidelity of Sita, Rama makes his excuses and, in company with Lakshmana and Sita, regains the city of Ayodhya, where he receives a very warm welcome. He is then crowned king.

The Ramayana

What has been said earlier about the Mahabharata also applies to the Ramayana. Here is the climax, Rama's encounter with Sita after his victory.

Sita, her limbs shrinking into herself with shyness, walked hesitantly with Vibishana and came near Rama. She covered her face with her upper cloth and in a faint voice called out: 'My lord!' Tears choked her voice and she could speak no more. Sita whose very life was Rama stood by and she looked at the dear face of her lord. There was immense affection in her eyes and there was happiness and a feeling of amazement that this happiness had finally come her way. Her sorrow was at an end and her eyes were drinking in the beauty of Rama with thirsty eyes which had long been aching for a sight of him.

Rama spoke. His voice was harsh and his words were cruel. He sounded angry and he looked at the gentle wife, his loving Sita who stood before him, and said: 'Devi, you have been rescued from the enemy. I killed him and rescued you. This was done to vindicate my honour and my reputation. It was my duty to fight the enemy and kill him and I did so. I have reached the utmost limit of fury and his offence against me has been punished in a proper manner. My insult and my enemy have both been wiped out together. My valour has been displayed to the world and my efforts have been rewarded. When there is danger to his reputation a man of honour should make every effort to wipe it out. Hanuman's achievement in leaping across the sea and his burning the city of Lanka were great tasks well executed. Vibhishana left his brother and came to me with a heart full of love and his attempts have not been in vain.'

Sita was listening to this long recital and she wondered why Rama's voice was lacking in warmth. She was looking like a frightened deer and her eyes were filled with tears. Rama looked at her and his anger grew, like fire which is fed on ghee poured into it as an oblation. His frown was dreadful and his eyes were strangely devoid of the affection meant for her, and only her.

He said: 'Sita, as I said before, unable to bear the insult offered by the enemy Ravana, I took up the task of killing him and I have done so. You have been rescued from him. Sita, I wish to impress on you one truth: this war, this killing of Ravana was undertaken by me because I am an upholder of Dharma and because I could not brook the insult to me and to the ancient house of the Ikshvibakus. I did not do all this for your sake. Your name has now a stain on it and it hurts me to look at you even as a bright light hurts the eyes of a man with a pain in his eyes.

You are at liberty to take leave of me and go where you will. There is nothing I owe you now that my task has been completed. Which honourable man will, with love, take home with him his wife who has been living in the house of his enemy for several months? I belong to a noble house, a very noble house, and it does not befit me to take you with me. You have been sought after by the sinful Ravana and his lecherous eyes. I have won fame by my actions and by my rescue of you. I am indifferent towards you. You can go away from here wherever you wish. I have explained to you my thoughts and my decision.'

Rama turned his angry eyes on her once and turned away. He spoke nothing after that.

Sita had never before heard such words from Rama and, trembling like a creeper caught in the wind, she stood silent with tears streaming from her eyes. Her heart was breaking with the words of Rama. Her head was bowed.

(version by Kamala Subramaniam, Bharatiya Vidya Bhavan, Bombay 1981)

As well as telling stories independent of the main action of the work, book seven (*Uttarakanda*) relates a second repudiation of Sita. Pregnant, she is banished, but is welcomed into the hermitage of Valmiki (the supposed author of the epic). She gives birth to two sons, Kusa and Lava. Many years later, when Rama is offering the horse-sacrifice, Valmiki appears in the company of two singers who are none other than Kusa and Lava. Learning that the two singers are his own sons, Rama asks for Sita to be sought. In a desire to bear witness to her fidelity, Sita summons the earth as witness, and asks it to welcome her into its depths if she has not lied. The earth then opens under her feet and swallows up the faithful woman. Having prepared for his succession by designating his two sons as his successors, Rama ascends to heaven and resumes his divine form as Vishnu.

Though attributed by a long tradition to Valmiki, who also appears several times in the work, the Ramayana cannot have been composed by a single author, since the three main versions of the text that we have today differ considerably. On the other hand, Valmiki was probably a brilliant compiler who was able to combine in one consecutive literary composition the sparse fragments of the epic handed down by oral tradition. Modern criticism has shown that sections I and VII, in which Rama is presented as an incarnation of Vishnu, are later, and have been subsequently grafted on to the main sections (II–VI). It is impossible to be specific about the date of the final redaction of the work, but the style, which is more refined and complex than that of the Mahabharata, has led some scholars to think that the Ramayana was developed towards the end of the period of the redaction of the Mahabharata. On the other hand, other scholars, using different criteria, think that the Ramayana is earlier than the great epic.

The intrigue of the Ramayana which can be summed up as the history of a war undertaken by the hero Rama to regain his spouse after her abduction by the king of the demons seems sufficient in itself. However, it has recently been demonstrated that the Ramayana is more than that. It is a poem which depends on mythical and theological structures with their roots deep in the Vedic world. Some of them link up with Indo-European patterns of thought.

The Ramayana has become exceptionally popular in India, in areas where Indian influence predominates, and even outside the Indian world. It has been translated into the main languages of India, and the great poet Tulsi-Das (1532–1623) adapted it in a Hindi version of more than 10,000 verses, the Ramacaritamanasa (literally 'The Lake of the Legends of Rama'); this still has considerable prestige in India. The influence of Ramaite literature has also extended to Buddhist and Jainist literature.

3. Puranic literature and the Tantras

The term Puranas (literally 'ancient [stories]') denotes a vast literature, sometimes likened to a 'fifth Veda', which brings together several types of text (legends, genealogies, treatises). Composed in classical verse *slokas* in a less refined language than that of the epic, this literature, which is difficult to date, developed over more than a millennium, roughly between the fourth and the fourteenth centuries CE, from a sometimes relatively ancient basis. According to tradition, the Puranas are the work of Vyasa. He is said to have composed them for those who are not 'twice born' and who cannot have access to the Veda, to enable them to share in the mysteries of salvation. In fact these texts come from the sphere of the court bards (*sutas*), a milieu very close to that in which epic was developed. Epic abounds to such a degree in the Puranic texts that it could be said that it finds a natural prolongation in them. In contrast to the epics, however, the epic matter of the Puranas is never developed into a consecutive story.

In Puranic literature a distinction is made between the great Puranas (*Mahapuranas*), numbering eighteen, the most important of which are the Vishnu Purana and the Bhagavata Purana, and the secondary Puranas (*Upapuranas*), which are also fixed at eighteen by the tradition (however, their number is far higher – they have been estimated at around 100). In addition, several local Puranas (*Sthalapurana*), exalting a particular holy place or sanctuary, are to be included.

According to an ancient tradition, 'five characteristics' (*panchalakshanas*) are thought to constitute the heart of the Puranas and to sum up their content. These are: the creation of the universe (*sarga*); its recreation after each periodical annihilation (*pratisarga*); the genealogy of the deities and saints (*vamsa*); the eras of humanity ruled by the Manu (*manvantara*); and the history of the royal dynasties (*vamsanucarita*). These Puranic 'characteristics', which some Puranas enlarge to ten (cf. Bhagavata Purana II, 10, 1), seem to have constituted the basic essentials of the Puranas. However, after successive additions, these *lakshanas* are far from exhausting the subject-matter of this literature. In it we find a good deal of other material dealing with ritual, religious philosophy, divination, and also secular matters like law, politics, grammar and measurement. Thus some Puranas become real encyclopaedias (in particular Agni Purana and Garuda Purana).

Partly because of their popular character, most of the Puranas are tied to the great religious families of Hinduism. Thus it is that one can talk of the Vishnuite Puranas (Vishnu, Bhagavata, Naradiya Purana) or the Shivaite Puranas (Shiva Skanda, Linga Purana). However, this link with one particular 'branch' or sect is never systematically stable. In fact each Vishnuite Purana contains praises or homage to Shiva and vice versa.

If the Puranas are intended for open and communal worship, the Tantras (literally 'chain of fabric' = doctrine) are addressed only to individuals who have been properly initiated. The term Tantras covers a considerable collection of magical and esoteric texts running counter to the way of renunciation (*samnyasa*), since they suggest a way of deliverance which integrates the powers of the body, thus reconciling enjoyment (*bhukti*) and deliverance (*mukti, moksha*).

Starting from learned connections between the microcosm and the macrocosm, the adept draws a series of parallels between the microcosm (the human being) and the macrocosm (the universe). In this system the primordial energy (*sakti*), identified with the female emanation of the deity Shiva, animates and supports the universe. This system of correlations between human beings and the universe also results in a mystical and subtle physiology which posits the oneness of this basic cosmic energy and vital force circulating in the human body in the form of 'breaths' (*pranas*) in canals (*nadis*), concentrated in six centres of consciousness in the body, spread along the cerebro-spinal axis and called *chakras* (literally 'wheels').

Explaining that by its act of manifestation this energy is in some way 'extended' from the supreme principle (Shiva), the Tantric texts say metaphorically that it is 'numbed' and that it remains coiled up like a serpent (literally, 'that which forms rings' [*kundala*], hence its name *kundalini*), in the first *chakra* called *muladhara* (literally 'basic support'), situated at the base of the vertebral column. Tantric yoga teaches that by appropriate means, which we cannot dwell on here, this energy can be aroused and thus ascend from *chakra* to *chakra* to the last, the *sahasrara* (this seventh *chakra* is not strictly a *chakra* but beyond the *chakra*), situated at the top of the skull and identified with the supreme transcendent lord (Paramashiva), a symbolic place where the union of Shiva and Shakti (*Shiva-shakti samarasya*) is realized, and the last stage of spiritual realization in which the adept achieves deliverance by uniting individualized energy and consciousness with the energy of the universal consciousness.

The Tantras equally emphasize the idea that the Absolute is sacred word (*vach*) and develop a mysticism of sound in which the magic syllables (*bijas*) and incantatory formulae (*mantras*) have an important place, notable in Tantric initiation. Visual supports in the form of diagrams (*yantras*) or symbolic images (*mandalas*) are also used as a basis for meditative exercises.

Without going into detail, we should note that the Tantras are distinguished from currents of Vishnuism called *samhita* (literally 'collection'); the Shivaite Tantras called *agamas* (literally 'traditions') and the Tantras of the adepts of the goddess Durga called Saktagamas. Furthermore, the Buddhist tradition also has its own Tantras. This type of text has been composed down to modern times.

II
Hindu Myths, Beliefs and Rites

The American scholar Mircea Eliade has described the transitional phase between the ancient form of Brahmanism (Vedism) and classical post-epic Hinduism as the 'Hindu synthesis'. In fact, this period during which new texts appeared, constituting the corpus of post-Vedic Hinduism (the post-Vedic Upanishads, the Puranas, epic texts, the Tantras), does display all the features of a period of 'synthesis'. During the millennium largely covering the period from the fifth century BCE to the fifth century CE, Brahmanism underwent an exceptional geographical expansion which brought it into contact with many indigenous cultures: it won over the east and south of the sub-continent and also expanded into several regions of South–East Asia (Ceylon, the Indo–Chinese peninsula, the Indonesian archipelago) in rivalry with Buddhism. Faced with the cultures which it encountered and perhaps even under pressure from them, Brahmanism found itself forced to assimilate certain local cults and to integrate the popular indigenous deities. This contributed towards enriching the Hindu pantheon. In the same period, reforms were made within Brahmanism itself, since the conquerors had to take a new element into account: the religious competition in the regions which had recently been Hinduized (mainly in the east) and which were opposed to Brahmanism. So it was that around the sixth century BCE, in the regions of Magadha (southern Bihar) in which Hinduization was both new and superficial, Buddhism and Jainism succeeded in demonstrating their differences and, a few centuries later, triumphed.

The fusion between the religious traditions which goes back to the Vedic sources and elements belonging to indigenous cultures (in particular Dravidian culture) finally transformed Brahmanic religion. What is now called 'Hinduism' is to some degree the result of this cultural synthesis, which began more than two thousand years ago. For lack of precise documents, we do not know the chronology of the main stages of the synthesis, and, as has already been indicated above, we can never see the transition between ancient Brahmanism and Hinduism. On the other hand, it is clear that at the end of this phase Hindu religion offers a new face. By comparison with Vedism, which was characterized by an extreme ritualism, Hinduism appears primarily as a tremendous spiritual current with its source in an authentic mystical experience. Generally speaking, it emphasizes the relationship between human beings and the divine more than Vedism. In classical Hinduism or the Hinduism of the sects, through the development of the doctrine of *bhakti*, the notion of personal faith, which is unknown to Vedism, makes itself felt: the faithful thus maintain a personal and privileged relationship with the deity who has been chosen to honour the family tradition, though without ceasing to revere other forms of the divine. So this deity becomes the 'chosen deity' (*ishta devata*), a preferred way of honouring the personified Absolute.

At the same time, the pantheon and the cult are also profoundly renewed at this point. Furthermore, Indian philosophy also begins a new phase of its history, since it is precisely around the beginning of the Christian era that the Brahmanic *darshanas* (literally 'perspectives [on the real]') begin to appear.

This chapter will offer a survey of the beliefs and cultural practices of Hinduism, followed by an account of the main lines of the development of Hindu religion during its classic (between the fourth and thirteenth centuries) and post-classic (between the thirteenth and eighteenth centuries) phases. The following chapter will deal with the modern and contemporary period, discussing the reform movements of the nineteenth century and the spiritual figures (gurus) in contemporary Hinduism.

1. A renewed pantheon

By the first centuries of the Christian era, the gods of the old Vedic pantheon had already lost their prestige and their power for some time. In the pantheon of post-Vedic Brahmanism, in effect they occupied only a secondary position, since from then on the essentials of the cult were organized around other deities, namely Vishnu, Shiva and Brahma. Furthermore, new divine figures made their entry into this renewed pantheon. Before we examine the new gods who were promoted, we should first look at what became of the Vedic deities in the framework of a Hinduism which was first epic, and then classic.

In the new pantheon, Indra, the invincible god of Vedic times, seems to keep his ascendancy over the other gods. However, his ancient prestige is largely

10. Agni, represented as a figure with two heads, evoking domestic fire and sacrificial fire. Here the god is portrayed with his animal support, the ram. Wooden sculpture, Dravidian (seventeenth century CE).

curtailed, which is why his privilege of leading the divine troop remains very theoretical. On the other hand, he is mentioned as head of the four (later eight) 'regents' (*astadikpalas*), who are also called *lokapalas*, i.e. 'regents of the world', or *dignathas*, 'protectors of the directions', deities charged with protecting the four points of the compass and the intermediate points in space. In this function, Indra is the regent of the east. Other Vedic deities fulfil the function of *lokapalas*: Yama for the south, Varuna for the west, Soma for the north-east, Vayu for the north-east, Agni for the south-east, and Surya for the south-west.

At the same time, Indra's function as god of the rains becomes more specific, as does his role as the god who is a magician. But he is still the god who pursues demons, all the more so since epic poetry elaborated his fight against the demon Vrtra. In iconography, Indra is generally represented as mounted on the elephant Airavata or on the chariot (*ratha*) Pushpaka driven by Matali, his faithful squire.

The figure of Indra has crossed the frontiers of Brahmanism to pass into Buddhism and Jainism. Under the name of Sakra (Pali Sakka), in Buddhism Indra becomes the head of a category of celestial beings, the *tavatimsa* (literally the 'thirty-two'), who watch over the cosmic order and protect the Buddhist law.

In the Vedic period, Agni was one of the most important deities in the pantheon, since fire was the heart of sacrifice. The further the development from the ancient period of Hindu religion, the more the figure of this god faded and became secondary. By contrast, down to the modern period Agni has remained one of the central figures of everyday domestic ritual.

Iconography has tended to anthropomorphize this divine figure. Depending on whether the focus is on his forms of sacrificial and domestic fire or his three modalities – heavenly fire (the sun), atmospheric fire (lightning) or earthly fire, Agni is represented in the form of a two-headed or three-headed figure with his hair caught up in a circle (of fire: *kesamandala*). The body of the deity is given seven arms bearing various attributes (trident, jar of ghee or sacred butter, etc.) and wearing the sacred

11. Ganesha, elephant-headed with his shakti (consort).

thread (*yajnopavita*). The ram (*aja*) is the mount (*vahana*) or the animal support of the god or the personified fire.

After what may strictly speaking be called the Vedic period, the two sovereign gods Mitra and Varuna very quickly fall into second place. Probably as a result of Iranian influences, the former becomes one of the divinized forms of the sun. At the beginning of the Christian era a cult of the Persian god Mithra developed even in the regions of north-west India under the name of Miiro. Varuna also lost his ancient prestige. He became a god of the waters, particularly those of the ocean, but his cult faded away quite rapidly.

Vayu, the god of wind, absorbed the Maruts. In epic poetry he is the 'breath' (*prana*), understood as the universal soul. As Pavana, he is also the father of Hanuman, the popular monkey god who is the companion of Rama in the Ramayana. Traditional iconography represents Vayu mounted on a gazelle (*mrga*).

As in Vedic times, Yama remains the sovereign of the empire of the dead, As Dharmaraja, that is, 'king of the law', he is the judge of souls, who punishes the wicked and distributes punishments and rewards. However, his mythology is difficult to reconcile with the doctrine of transmigration, since everything is determined by *karma*. Moreover, the one who is also called Mrityu, 'death', is presented surrounded with assistants who are none other than time (*kala*) or the demons of illness. Other Vedic deities (Dyaus, Pushan, Sruya, the Asvins) also belong to this renewed pantheon, but only play a secondary role.

Alongside divine figures going back to the origins of Vedism, the post-Vedic Hindu pantheon also includes 'younger' deities (although some of them are mentioned episodically in Vedic texts): Ganesha, Kama, Kubera and Skanda.

In Hinduism, Ganesha or Ganapati (literally the 'lord of the *ganas*' [*devatas*] = divine troops) becomes the 'Lord of obstacles' (Vighnesvara), who smoothes the way in any human enterprise (trade, journeys . . .) but more particularly in the world of letters, which is why he is often invoked before the beginning of literary work. It seems that originally this figure had been connected with fertility. Since he is well typed by iconography, he is easily recognizable: with an elephant head, he has only one tusk, which gives him the epithet *ekadanstra*. Furthermore, he has a prominent abdomen, which gives him the title *lambodara* ('with a fat belly'), an indication that probably he was originally a *yaksha*. His traditional mount is the mouse, an animal known for getting through obstacles and also in connection with agriculture, because it destroys the crops. Among the characteristic attributes which he holds in his four hands one usually finds a broken tusk, a lotus, an axe and a rice cake.

12. Ganesha, monolith on the terrace of Hoysalesvara temple, Halebid, Karnataka, South India.

Kama, god of love and more particularly of desire and sexual love, has Vedic antecedents, since *kama*, the force personifying cosmic desire, is presented in Hymn X, 129 of the Rig Veda as the catalytic element of the cosmogonic process. The Vedic texts mention this notion several times, and the Atharva

Veda dedicates a long hymn to Kama (IX, 2). However, it is only from the period of the epics that Kama becomes a divine figure with his mythology and well-defined attributes. Like the Roman Cupid, the god of love is represented with a bow and arrows which he fires to kindle the desire of gods and human beings. Having disturbed the meditation of Shiva, inflaming him with desire for Parvati, he was consumed by the fire of the third eye of the ascetic god, which is why Kama is supposed not to have a body (*ananga*). However, aware of the distress of the goddess Rati, spouse of Kama, Shiva allowed the god of love to take another body in which, according to other sources, he resuscitated him in the form of Pradyumna, whom certain legends present as the son of Krishna. The parrot (*suka*) is the animal support of Kama. Among his attributes are the bow of sugar cane (*iksukodanda*), the string of which is made by a row of bees, and five arrows (*pancasara*) thought to be made of five different flowers to which mythology has given special names. Mention is also made of a banner with the representation of a mythological marine animal (*makara*), resembling a crocodile but often likened to a dolphin.

By contrast, Kubera appears only at the end of Vedic times. Before becoming the god of wealth, he seems first to have been honoured as head of the *yakshas*, the inoffensive genies already known to Vedic mysticism. Some sources also make Kubera the *lokapala* charged with watching over the north. Iconography represents him in the form of a white dwarf with a fat belly. In some representations he is given three feet, three heads and one eye. His main distinguishing feature is a purse which he carries on him and which is thought to contain nine 'treasures' (*nidhi*), including the lotus and the conch.

Skanda, god of war and leader of the army of the gods, has a large number of epithets emphasizing his different qualities. In direct connection with his warlike function, Skanda is called Mahasena, the 'great captain'. Later, he was to become the chief of

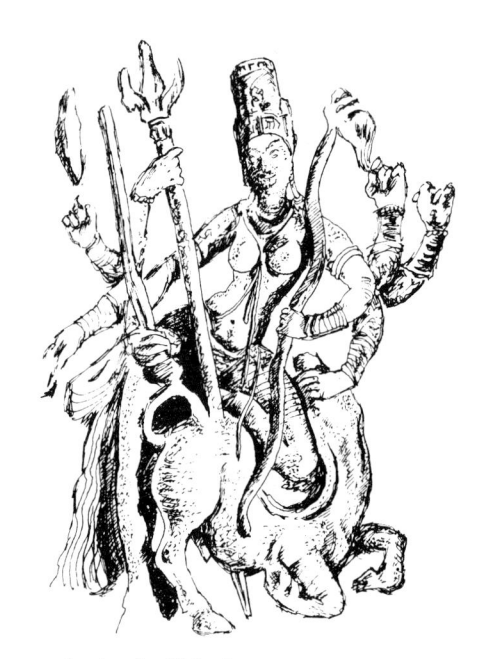

13. Durga slaying buffalo demon

the demons of sickness, particularly those affecting children, and the patron of thieves. His main attributes are the 'banner of victory' and 'peacock's feathers'.

To all the deities that I have just listed are added further figures of Vedic origin or of a later date, some even of non-Aryan origin: divine heroes, important female deities (Durga, *shakti* [literally 'energy'] of Shiva in multiple names and forms [Kali, Parvati, etc.]; Lakshmi, spouse of Vishnu; Radha, spouse of Krishna), and fantastic animals, to which Hindu mythology attributes a specific function. However, it is around the great figures of Vishnu, Shiva and Brahma that the great themes of Hindu mythology crystallize.

Vishnu, Shiva and Brahma, who dominate the pantheon of classical and post-classical Hinduism, very soon came to be grouped in a triad. In one of the latest Vedic Upanishads, the Maitri Upanishad (V, 2), the three deities are related to the theology of the *gunas* (literally 'quality', 'attributes') of *samkhya*,

14. Kali

a philosophy of enumeration which assumes the task of listing and classifying the twenty-five 'principles' (*tattvas*) or constituents on which the world of phenomena is based.

According to *samkhya*, phenomenal reality unfolds by the interaction of two main ontological principles. On the one hand is fundamental nature (*prakrti*) or the pre-established, from which proceed, by evolution, intellect (*buddhi*) and the function of the ego (*ahamkara*), this latter in turn producing the five organs of perception, the thinking faculty (*manas*), the five organs of action, and then the subtle elements (*tanmatra*), from which derive the coarser elements (space, fire, air, water, earth), the combinations of which form the material universe. On the other hand are the spiritual monads (of an infinite number but identical and distinct only numerically) or Spirit (*purusha*) considered in the purity of its essence and independently of its possible modes of incarnation: human, animal or divine. Furthermore, *samkhya* postulates that, contrary to the spiritual monads, primordial nature is affected by three 'qualities' or attributes (*gunas*) which preserve a balance far from the presence of the *purusha*. It distinguishes 1. *sattva* (literally, that which has the character of being [*sat*]), representing the brightest and lightest element of nature; 2. *rajas* (literally dust), corresponding to the active element; 3. *tamas*, which relates to a principle of darkness, heaviness and inertia. The approach of the spiritual monads destroys the equilibrium of the three *gunas* and sets nature in motion, the action of *purusha* on *prakrti* being comparable to that of a catalyst, since *purusha* is inactive. The system functions as it is and does not have the intervention of any divine transcendent regulating power.

In the Maitri Upanishad, Brahma is identified with *rajas*, Vishnu with *sattva*, and Shiva, called by his ancient name Rudra, with *tamas*. Later, the term *trimurti* (literally, the three forms [of the divine]), coined originally in Shivaite circles, systematizes this divine triad. The *trimurti* associates each of its elements with one of the cosmic activities and functions as follows: Brahma 'emits' the world, and represents the process of creation (*srsti*); Vishnu assures its sustenance and represents the process of conservation (*sthiti*); finally, Shiva destroys it and represents the process of dissolution (*pralaya*), a cycle which continues indefinitely.

Despite his prestigious name, Brahma is far from being the most important god in the *trimurti*. He is the product of a long process of speculation on the impersonal *brahman* of Vedic thought, being given a life of his own only to the degree that this abstract notion allows it. In all India he has only one independent temple, that of Pushkar, north-west of Ajmer in Rajasthan, which each year in the full moon of the month of Karttik (October–November) becomes an important place of pilgrimage, attracting thousands of the faithful. His functions are connected with the process of creation, since it is he who organizes the universe; hence the epithet Pitamha (literally 'great father [creator]'). In the same way, he is also called Svayambhu (literally, 'the one who exists by himself'). In fact he absorbed the functions formerly exercised by Brihaspati, Prajapati and Visvakarma. Iconography usually represents him mounted on a swan or sometimes on a chariot drawn by seven swans. His representa-

15. Brahma at Huccappyagudi temple, Aihole, Karnataka, South India (sixth century CE)

tion in the form of a deity with four faces – representing the four Vedas, the four *varnas*, the four ages of the world (*yugas*) – or turned towards the four points of the compass is very common.

If the Rig Veda devotes only six hymns to Vishnu (five of which are shared with another deity), from the beginning of Vedism this divine figure nevertheless enjoyed much greater importance than might be supposed from the text. Counted among the *adityas* by the Rig Veda, Vishnu is often mentioned as a solar deity. In his heyday, his mythology was summed up in the 'three steps' (*trivikrama*) which he took to create the world and measure the universe (see Rig Veda I, 154 and Satapatha Brahmana I, 2, 5, 1). These divine strides relate to the extreme points of the course of the sun (rising, zenith, setting). Another feature of the personality of Vishnu emphasized by the Vedic texts is his friendship for Indra, a god who also helps him in his work. It is for Indra that he holds up the heavens, and for him that he opens up space with his steps so that Indra has a new arena for crushing the dragon Vrtra.

The prestige of Vishnu did not cease to grow, since this deity successively took on functions performed at other times by other gods, notably Indra and Brahma-Prajapati. In the Brahmanas, Vishnu is identified with sacrifice (cf. Satapatha Brahmana XIV, 1). Furthermore it is by repeating his triple step and identifying himself with it that the person offering a sacrifice can attain heaven.

In epic literature, in which he appears frequently, Vishnu is always represented as a benevolent god. Iconography regularly portrays him in mediation

16. Brahma the creator, facing four directions

17. Lord Vishnu and his attributes

during the interval corresponding to the dissolution of the world (*pralaya*) which separates two successive creations. In his representations, he can be seen lying on the serpent Sesha (or Ananta) with a thousand heads, which floats on the surface of the cosmic waters. During this mystic sleep, Vishnu meditates on the world; at his 'awakening', a lotus issues from his nostril, bearing Brahma, to whom the function of creator is then allotted. As protector of the worlds and the universe, Vishnu assures their permanence, and as the guardian of *dharma*, he appears periodically to re-establish the good when the world is troubled by disorder. He then 'descends' to earth to restore order and relieve humankind from disorder.

There are many modes of manifestation (*vibhutis*) by which Vishnu enters into relation with phenomenal reality. I shall mention just the two main ones, the *vyuhas* (literally emanation, expansion = hypostasis) and the *avataras* (literally '[divine] descent') or avatars, also called *vibhava* ('manifestation').

The 'four *vyuhas*' (*chaturvyuha*) constitute the regular manifestations of Vishnu, which are directly linked to the cosmic process. This doctrine, which was developed and then disseminated by one of the oldest schools of Vishnuism, the Pancaratra movement, took shape during the very first centuries of our era. By reason of the complexity of the doctrine, only its outline can be presented here.

On the four *vyuhas* is superimposed the *paramarupa* (literally, the supreme form), that is, the supreme godhead in its infinity, which escapes all definition and resides in the Vaikuntha, the paradise of Vishnu. This 'supreme' Absolute manifests itself at the beginning of each creation by its eternal form, the *nityavibhuti* (literally, eternal manifesta-

18. Vishnu reclining on the serpent Ananta after the universal dissolution (*mahapralaya*) between two 'creations'. Granite relief from the Mahisasuramardini Mandapa at Mamallapuram, Mahabalipuram, Tamil Nadu (first half of seventh century CE). On the left, note the hooded heads of the serpent.

tion), which in personal form is also Vasudeva, the possessor of six divine 'qualities' (*gunas*): knowledge, energy, power, strength, efficacy, vigour.

When the god becomes demiurge, he 'splits' into three hypostases, each inheriting two of the six divine 'qualities' while being present in each of them: Samkarsana, which inherits the attributes of knowledge and energy, presides at creation; Pradyumna, which bears the attributes of power and strength, preserves the universe; Aniruddha, which has the attributes of efficacy and vigour, exercises the function of destroyer. Besides their role in the cosmic process, the three hypostases emanating from Vasudeva also exercise a moral activity. It will have been noted that the three *vyuhas* relate to the three figures of the Shivaite *trimurti*. Later texts gave each of the *vyuhas* secondary manifestations, each of which fulfils other particular functions.

When this first stage or 'pure emanation' (*suddhasrsti*) ends, the process of the organization of the universe undergoes a second phase in the course of which the three last *vyuhas* manifest their creative activity. The following stage is that of inferior creation following evolution and the interaction of *prakrti* and *purusha*. Then, arising from Vishnu's nostril, there appears the cosmic eye which contains the universe.

The second of the two main modes of manifestation (*vibhutis*) of Vishnu, the *avatara* (from the prefix *ava-* indicating a movement from above downwards and the root *tr-* 'traverse' = *avatara* = 'divine descent'), is a partial or complete incarnation of the lord in the form of an animal or a being in human form. The term avatar, which is applied in the first place to the 'incarnations' of Vishnu – although the Vishnuite Samhitas tend rather to use the term *vibhava* (literally manifestation) – equally characterizes the modes of manifestation of his consort Lakshmi, and those of other Brahmanic figures like Agni or Vayu. Furthermore, the saints and gurus have often been credited with being avatars of a particular deity. This procedure has made it possible for certain great figures of myth or history to be divinized. The popularity of the notion of the avatar thus quickly went beyond the framework of Vishnuism, since the Shivaite tradition also accepted avatars of Shiva. It is probable that the systematization by the Vishnuite schools of the ancient notion of avatar influenced and then contaminated other religious traditions.

The coming of an avatar is always occasional. There is nothing obligatory about it, and it intervenes only by a free act of the lord when *dharma* is threatened by subversive forces disturbing the order of things and there is a risk that the world will come to ruin. The classic scheme of the avatar is given by Krishna, the full incarnation of Vishnu, in the Bhagavad Gita.

After emphatically stating the eminently immutable nature of the divine – the text says that it is 'not

---

The Scheme of Avatars

Krishna:

Although I am unborn, everlasting, and I am the Lord of all, I come to my realm of nature and through my wondrous power I am born.

When righteousness is weak and faints and unrighteousness exults in pride, then my Spirit arises on earth.

For the salvation of those who are good, for the destruction of evil in men, for the fulfilment of the kingdom of righteousness, I come to this world in the ages that pass.

He who knows my birth as god and who knows my sacrifice, when he leaves his mortal body, goes no more from death to death, for he in truth comes to me.

How many have come to me, trusting in me, filled with my Spirit, in peace from passions and fears and anger, made pure by the fire of wisdom!

(Bhagavad Gita IV, 6–10)

---

born' and has an imperishable essence – and the supremacy of the divine, Krishna indicates to Arjuna that it is the divine itself which descends to earth in his own form ('using my nature'). The text then presents the reason for this manifestation: it is the decline of *dharma* and the growth in this world of 'vice' (*adharma*) which provokes the coming of the avatar. The eighth verse shows what could be called the divine plan or design: the avatar descends to protect the good (*sadhu*), destroy the bad (*dusktra*), and re-establish the cosmic and moral order. The last verse indicates the final aim of the manifestation: belief in the avatar frees the faithful from the cycle of rebirths (*samsara*).

The number of 'incarnations' of Vishnu given by the texts is very variable. In the earliest sources it is usually only four or six. Later texts mention more important numbers: six, twenty-two, twenty-three, twenty-four, even thirty-nine avatars. Only at a very late stage (around the tenth century) was a classical list finally established giving 'ten avatars', related to the cyclical law of the ages (*yugas*) of the present creation.

A. Avatars of the first age (*krita yuga*), literally 'age accomplished'

1. Matysa or Matsyavatara, the 'incarnation in the form of the fish'

Mentioned for the first time in the Satapatha Brahmana (1, 8, 1) and related with some variants by several Puranas, the legend of Matysa is linked with the Indian version of the flood. Here are the broad outlines of the version in the Satapatha Brahmana.

When he is performing his ablutions, the seventh Manu, founder and legislator of present humanity, sees a little fish appear in the water. It asks him for help and protection. It announces to Manu that one day it will save him from great peril, an immense flood which will carry off all the creatures on earth. The fish tells Manu to build an ark to escape this catastrophe. Manu heeds the little fish, builds his boat and prepares to follow the advice of the fish, which is growing. When he no longer has any containers in which to hold the fish, he throws it back into the sea. The moment the flood covers the earth, Manu gets into the ark and moors it to a fin of the fish, which leads him to the mountains of the north. When he gets there Manu is saved; he offers a sacrifice of milk, butter and cream from which, at the end of a year, he produces a woman with whom he repeoples the earth.

Another version of this legend reported by the Bhagavata Purana is that the fish Vishnu manifests itself to recover from the bottom of the ocean the Veda which the demon Hayagriva had stolen from Brahma. One of the epithets of Vishnu is Hayagrivaripu, i.e. the '[victorious] enemy of Hayagriva'.

19. Vishnu with his tortoise avatar at the churning of the ocean

2. Kurma or Kurmavatara, the 'incarnation in the form of the tortoise'

Linked to the previous avatar, the tortoise allows the gods to discover at the bottom of the ocean ambrosia (*amrta*) and treasures submerged by a deluge. Traditional iconography often represents Vishnu-tortoise at the bottom of the ocean, his back serving as a pedestal for Mount Mandara, which *devas* and *asuras* use for churning; this is the 'churning of the ocean of milk' (*ksirodamathana*). A number of marvellous things come out of the churned waves, in particular Dhanvantari, the physician of the gods, but also the goddess Lakshmi, *soma* and the Apsaras.

3. Varaha or Varahavatara, the 'incarnation in the form of the wild boar'

Taking the form of a wild boar, Vishnu saves the earth, which had been submerged in the ocean by the demon Hiranyaksha.

4. Narasimha or Nrsimahavatara, the 'incarnation in the form of the man-lion'

The last avatar to descend in the course of the first age of the present humanity, the fourth incarnation of Vishnu, serves as an intermediary between the zoomorphic incarnations and the future incarnations, all in human form. Taking the form of a creature who is half man and half lion, Vishnu succeeds in killing the younger *daitya* (a category of enemies of the gods) brother Hiranyaksha, called Hiranyakashipu.

Hiranyakashipu had practised a long and rigorous asceticism, drinking only water for 11,500 years, and had made a vow of silence. One day he received a visit from Brahma, who granted him a wish. Hiranyakashipu put it like this: he asked Brahma to ensure that he, Hiranyakashipu, was not killed either by a god or a demon, whatever its rank, by a domestic animal or a wild animal, by a bird or a reptile, by a hand-held weapon or a missile, by day or by night, inside or outside his palace. The wish met with the approval of Brahma, who disappeared into space with his troop. Thinking that he was invincible, the *daitya* began to subjugate the creatures and to disturb the calm of the ascetics. Having cast down the gods from their thrones, he finally ensured his domination over the three worlds and installed himself in the empyrean. The gods then intervened with Lord Vishnu for justice to be done. Assuming a body which was half-man and half-lion, and rising in the twilight (between day and night) from a pillar of the palace in a cloud of glory, the man-lion destroyed the demon with his bare hands.

B. **Avatars of the second age, *treta yuga*, literally 'age of the triad'**

5. Vamana or Vamanavatara, the 'incarnation [in the form of the] dwarf'

Taking the form of a dwarf, Vishnu saves the world from the demon Bali, a *daitya* (a category of *asura*)

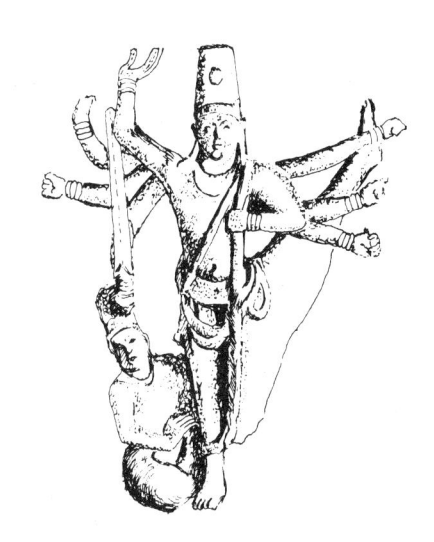

20. Vishnu's three strides and his dwarf avatar

who has come to reign over the worlds of creation. Sent by the gods to Bali, Vishnu asks Bali to grant him a piece of land that he can cover in three leaps. When Bali agrees, Vishnu resumes his normal size and in three leaps covers all creation, thus freeing it from the yoke of Bali.

6. Parasurama or Parasumavatara, the 'incarnation [in the form of] Rama with the axe'

This sixth avatar marks the beginning of a new category of incarnations, that of the divinized heroes.

Rama saves the world from the tyranny of the class of Kshatriyas (noble warriors) who have usurped the authority of the Brahmins, thus threatening the collapse of society. Armed with his axe, Rama exterminates all the warriors and re-establishes the spiritual primacy of the Brahmins. To explain why some Kshatriyas still exist, the texts say that these are the children which the Brahmins had by the widows of the Kshatriyas who were exterminated. After these exploits, Parasurama withdraws to Mount Mahendra, there to lead a solitary life (Mahabharata III, 118, 13–14). With this figure, the notion of avatar is somewhat misused, since the incarnate one does not rejoin the divine world after accomplishing his mission. That is why Parsurama is sometimes presented as an *avesa* of Vishnu, i.e. an incarnation of a lower degree.

7. Rama or Ramachandra

This central figure of the Ramayana is the very type of the divinized hero. It seems that his divinization was gradual and took place in several stages. In a first stage Rama is compared to Vishnu, and then becomes a 'particle' (*amsa*) of this deity before being identified completely with him, to become a total incarnation (*purnavatara*) of Vishnu. Rama is the paragon of the just kind and an indefatigable foe of demons: he eliminates the redoubtable Ravan, leader of the *rakshasas*.

C. Avatars of the third age, *dvapara yuga*, literally 'age [characterized by the] two': only half the original *dharma* remains

8. Krishna

Krishna (literally the 'black' or the 'dark' one, by virtue of the dark blue colour of his skin) is the most famous of the avatars of Vishnu, the one who has most crystallized popular devotion and also contributed to the development of the Vishnuite cult. He is seen as being the total manifestation of Vishnu, since he assumes the human condition completely. He was born in Mathura (in the state of Uttar Pradesh), in a Kshatriya family of the clan of Yadava. However, in order to avoid the persecutions of his uncle, king Kansa, at his birth he was entrusted to a shepherd called Nandagopa. He knew the joys of childhood, grew up, and fulfilled his missions to the end, before being killed by a wound on the heel from the arrow of a hunter. His death inaugurates the fourth age, the *kali yuga* (literally 'the evil age'), which according to Indian astrologers began in 3102 BCE. After his earthly death, the avatar Krishna returned to heaven where he regained his divine form.

21. Krishna dancing on the defeated serpent Kaliya

The mighty deeds of Krishna are related in an abundant hagiographical literature, particularly in the supplement to the Mahabharata, the Harivansa (literally, 'genealogy of Hari' = Vishnu), which relates his childhood adventures in detail, and in several Puranas (notably the Bhagavata, book X, and the Vishnu Purana). However, despite this abundant literary material, the origins of this deity remain obscure.

In fact these texts contain legends probably from different sources, which perhaps do not always speak of the same god but intertwine in an attempt to form a single framework. Some joins are evident.

There are several Krishnas, or rather there is one Krishna with several facets.

1. There is the mischievous god-child (Balakrishna or Damodara) who causes his adoptive father Nandagopa and his wife torments when they are staying in the camp in the forest of Mahavana

22. Infant Balakrishna

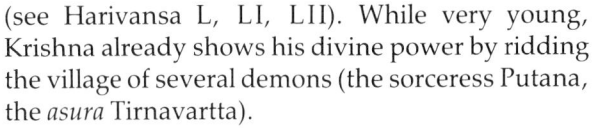

23. Krishna Gopala playing his flute

(see Harivansa L, LI, LII). While very young, Krishna already shows his divine power by ridding the village of several demons (the sorceress Putana, the *asura* Tirnavartta).

2. There is the adolescent herdsman god (Krishna-Gopala) of the forest of Vrindaban who plays the flute (Krishna Venugopala) and, surrounded by shepherdesses (*gopi*), dances the 'game of *rasa*' (*rasalila*) with his favourite Radha, a divine game which in the Krishna tendency constitutes a real mystery.

3. There is the god who defeats the Kansa, whom he kills at Mathura, and the founder of the city of Dvaraka (present day Dwarka, in the state of Gujarat).

4. There is the god of the Bhagavad Gita and the charioteer of Arjuna who advises the Pandavas and makes them triumph over their enemies and cousins, the Kauravas.

One could schematize the major lines of development of the figure of Krishna as follows: at first a simple pastoral deity from the countryside around Mathura, Krishna was then identified with the hero Krishna of the Bhagavad Gita before becoming one of the avatars of Vishnu, and then the most important of them. As for his cult, we move successively from a local circumscribed local cult to a *bhakti* which proceeds to the necessary identifications and then, at a later stage, to a *bhakti* which has become sectarian: this engenders new 'movements' (*sampradayas*) which no longer make Krishna a form of Vishnu but identify him with the supreme god and master of the universe, even speaking of 'incarnations' of Krishna and thus making Vishnu a secondary aspect of Krishna. This is the case with the religious movement inaugurated in the sixteenth century in Bengal by Visvambhara Misra (1486–1533), in religion Sri Krishna Chaitanya (*chaitanya* = consciousness → Krishna, absolute consciousness), which was directly taken up by A. C. Bhaktivedanta (Swami Pabhupada, 1896–1977), the founder of the International Society for Krishna Consciousness.

Alongside the adventures of Krishna, the Krishnaite tradition has also retained several episodes from the life of his son Pradyumna and his grandson Aniruddha.

24. Krishna the divine herdsman, playing the flute. Wooden sculpture from a processional chariot (seventeenth century CE)

D. Avatars of the fourth age, *kali yuga*, literally the 'evil age'

9. Buddha

The ninth avatar, Siddharta Gautama (c.566–486 BCE), is the figure of the historical Buddha, recovered from the Vishnuite tradition so as better to reintegrate his adversaries within Hinduism. The mention of Buddha as Vishnu's avatar in the traditional lists probably goes back to the end of the seventh century, a period of tension between the adherents of Vishnuism, who attempted to reconvert their adversaries and rivals to Hinduism, and the Buddhists. Vishnu was incarnate in Buddha so as definitively to abolish the bloody sacrifices of animals (*ahimsa* = 'absence of the desire to kill [*himsa*] and to harm' is the first of the 'five rules of ethical conduct' [*pancasila*] for all practising Buddhists) and to hasten the fall of the wicked.

10. Kalki (or Kalkin)

The avatar of the future, Kalki will be manifested at the end of the cosmic cycle when the *kali yuga* is ended and *dharma* has been entirely destroyed. He will come to punish the wicked and reward the good, destroy the present world and bring in a new golden age.

This tenth incarnation is represented either as a being with the head of a horse and the body of a man, or as a man mounted on a white horse (Kalkin = local form Karkin, 'the one who has a white horse' [*karka*]).

Beside these ten incarnations which have been described as indications of the power of Lord Vishnu, there are a series of important minor avatars described by the Bhagavata Purana and the other Vishnuite Puranas.

Embodying within the *trimurti* the process of dissolution (*pralaya*) and destruction of the universe, Shiva is the third major deity of this renewed pantheon.

25. Bhairava: Shiva in his terrible form

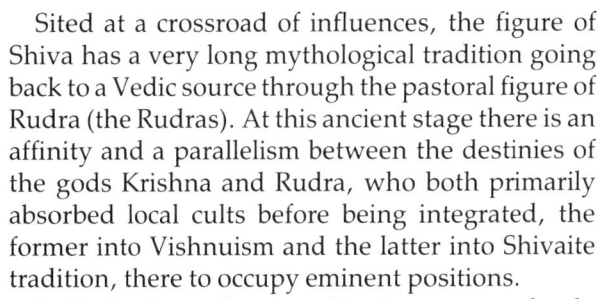

26. Shiva as Bhairava with skulls

Sited at a crossroad of influences, the figure of Shiva has a very long mythological tradition going back to a Vedic source through the pastoral figure of Rudra (the Rudras). At this ancient stage there is an affinity and a parallelism between the destinies of the gods Krishna and Rudra, who both primarily absorbed local cults before being integrated, the former into Vishnuism and the latter into Shivaite tradition, there to occupy eminent positions.

In Vedic times, the term *shiva* is as yet used only as an adjective signifying the 'benevolent' or the 'auspicious'; it is used as a euphemistic epithet to attract his favours and propitiate a group of disturbing deities, the Rudras, whose name is not to be spoken. As we have seen, this group of eleven gods led by Rudra embraces the idea of a formidable god, master of animals (*pasupati*) and nature, an eminently ambiguous figure whose fierce character is feared, though at the same time his power of healing is revered. In a later Vedic Upanishad, the Svetasvatara Upanishad (section III), Rudra accedes to the divine supremacy. Under the name Shiva he becomes the supreme god 'who dominates these worlds by his domination' (III.2). He creates and protects all beings and swallows them up at the end of time.

The cult of Shiva became established at the beginning of the epic period. In the literature of this period and in the Puranas, the figure of Shiva takes on increasing importance and he ends by becoming a deity of the first order. The Shivaite Puranas (notably the Shiva and Linga Puranas), which develop myths and traditions relating to Shiva, contributed very widely to the expansion of Shivaism. The more doctrinal speculations and the aspects of the cult were consigned to other collections, the *agamas* (literally 'traditions') from the beginning of the Christian era.

The affinity between the Vedic Rudra and Shiva is certain, the latter having absorbed a large part of the functions formerly attributed to Rudra. Like Rudra, Shiva is a very ambiguous deity, and his ambivalence also appears in his different names, which can be classified under two headings, each expressing one of the two faces of the deity. A first group of epithets brings out his formidable and violent character (*ugramurti*) and his role as destroyer within the *trimurti*. He is called Aghora, the 'non-terrible' (a euphemism), but also Bhairava, 'the terrible'; Hara, the 'seizer'; Kala, 'time [which destroys] – death'; Ugra, the 'fierce one'. Shiva is a violent god who is thought to haunt the places of cremation accompanied by his cohort of macabre assistants (vampires and wandering dead). Because he is the lord of destruction and the master of time, traditional iconography has counted the necklace of human skulls (*mundamala*) and the belt of cobras (*sarpamala*) among his main attributes.

27. Triune image of Shiva as the great god

In connection with his destructive function, Shiva is also called the 'king of the dance' (Nataraja) or 'lord of the dance' (Natesa or Natesvara). The Shivaite texts describe several kinds of dances practised by the lord Shiva, but the *ananda-tandava* (literally 'dance of happiness'), the cosmic dance *par excellence*, best sums up the function of Shiva Nataraja. This dance symbolizes the endless processes of the destruction and creation of the world, the cycle of manifestations and dissolutions of the cosmos and final deliverance. This aspect of Shiva has always been depicted by Indian iconography, notably by the magnificent bronzes of the Chola period (ninth to thirteenth centuries). Standing on a lotus pedestal, Shiva, represented with four arms, executes his dance while crushing with his right foot the dwarf demon Apasmara, while his raised left foot indicates the path of deliverance (*moksha*). In his upper raised right hand he holds a small sand drum (*damaru*) which calls the worlds into existence, and in his left hand a fiery torch which announces their destruction. The second of his right hands sketches a gesture of protection, the 'absence of fear' (*abhaya-hasta-mudra*), while the left hand points to the raised left foot (the refuge of the soul). The whole figure is often surrounded by a crown of flames (*prabha mandala*) springing from the pedestal.

28. Shiva contemplating as the master of all wisdom

At the opposite extreme to this terrible and destructive aspect, Shiva – whose name, we should recall, means 'benevolent' – is also a peaceful and protective deity, who heals and restores, as is emphasized by other appellations, notably Sankara, the 'giver of joy' and Sambhu, the 'auspicious'. Furthermore, a number of mythological episodes from the texts of the epics or the Puranas present him in a favourable light, calming suffering here and bringing happiness there.

In a related key, Shiva is also the god of life. His sign *par excellence* is the *linga* (literally mark, sign), which cannot be reduced just to a simply phallic emblem, as has long happened in the West. A re-reading of the myth on the 'origin of the *linga*' (*lingodbhava*) related in one of the most important Shivaite Puranas, the Linga Purana (1, 17, 5–52), allows us to see the meaning of this symbol of Shiva (Shivalinga) more clearly. The text relates how one day a struggle between Brahma and Vishnu broke out following a discussion, in the course of which the two gods could not agree on which of them was

29. Shiva Natarja – Lord of the dance

30a. Shiva linga at the sanctuary of Gudimallam, Andhra Pradesh. Carved on the lower part of a particularly realistic phallic symbol, the god is represented standing on a *yaksha* who has been identified with the demon Apasmara.

30b. Shiva Natarja. Indian bronze (eleventh century CE)

the greatest. Suddenly, as if to make them agree, an immense *linga* of fire appeared before them in the form of a column 'rich with a thousand crowns of flames, equal to one hundred fires (of the end) of time, without diminution or growth, without beginning, middle or end, incomparable, indomitable, indefinable, the first source of all things'. Surprised, Vishnu then suggested to Brahma that together they should search out the causes of this strange phenomenon. The former then transformed himself into a wild boar and began to root out the soil with his tusk to get to the very base of the column. Brahma transformed himself into a wild goose and flew into the sky to examine the upper point of the *linga*. After long research proved vain, the two gods ended up by prostrating themselves before this *linga*, i.e. before Shiva, recognizing that they had both been led astray by the power of illusion of the supreme lord. In the awareness of the faithful, the *linga* does not have a phallic, far less erotic, character; it represents the supreme Lord, the god of gods, greater than Brahma and Vishnu, the immovable axis of the world, the cosmic pillar (*sthanu*) without beginning or end, itself a symbol of the divine infinite and the image of a god who, although outside time, manifests himself to save his faithful.

There is a great variety of types of *linga*. First we can distinguish the natural *linga* (*svayambhuva linga*, literally '*linga* existing by itself'), usually in stone, exceptionally in ice, like that in the cave of Amarnath in Kashmir, regarded as spontaneous manifestations of Lord Shiva, and the other made by human hands and divided into several sub-categories. These are given the common appellation *mansalinga*, literally '*lingas* established by human beings'. In addition to those present in Shivaite sanctuaries, of which they form the heart, one can also find *lingas* on the family altars of all Shivaite believers, and some of the faithful (the *lingayat*) carry a *linga* on them, as the Shiva Purana recommends. The Shivaite Puranas list twelve 'primordial *lingas*' (*adilingas*) thought to manifest twelve aspects of Shiva and spread over twelve holy places.

31. Shiva and his consort Parvati on a lotus flower

Generally speaking, a *linga* takes the form of a cylinder of variable width standing on a square or circular plinth and made of stone or wood, sometimes metal, or moulded in clay, often with the upper tip rounded. Though it is often aniconic (without images), this cylinder can be decorated with certain motifs, notably engraved lines, the *brahma sutras* (literally 'thread of Brahma') or faces representing different aspects of Shiva; in this case the *linga* is said to be *mukhalinga* (literally *linga* with faces). When two lingas are put side by side in a sanctuary, the second shows the presence of Parvati, the consort of Shiva.

In sanctuaries, the *linga* is usually associated with a second element, the *yoni* (literally vulva), which serves as a kind of plinth or pedestal or envelops it like a trough capable of receiving liquid offerings. The association of the *linga* and the *yoni* should not be reduced to the image of divine coitus. Above all it represents Ardhanarisvara, the androgynous Shiva, who symbolizes the union of the two ontological principles which constitute the cosmos (*purusha* and *prakritri*) at the moment when the supreme being makes it arise from its latency.

Another aspect of Shiva combines in a paradox-

32. Linga and Yoni

ical way both asceticism (*tapas*) and sexuality or eroticism. From the discovery at Mohenjo-Daro of a steatite seal representing an ithyphallic figure (with an erect penis) surrounded by animals and seated with thighs open and legs folded back (see p.4), Sir John Marshall, one of the discoverers of the cities of the Indus, formulated the hypothesis that this figure was Shiva Pasupati in a yoga attitude, thus giving credence to the theory of a pre-Aryan substratum of yoga and the god Shiva. Today this hypothesis is not totally convincing, since in the remains of the cities of the Indus a certain number of long conical stones have been found which evoke the *lingas* of Shivaism; there is nothing specifically yogic about the posture depicted on the seal (a figure sitting on his haunches), and it could, for example, be the position of a craftsman (cobbler). So it is difficult to identify with certainty the posture represented on the seal as a yogic posture. Furthermore, if Shiva is given the title of Pasupati, it is because he is the lord of herds and cattle, while the animals surrounding the hypothetical proto-Shiva of Mohenjo-Daro are fawns. On the other hand, it is true that the Rig Veda twice mentions the cult of the phallus (VII, 21, 5; X, 99, 3) as the characteristic of the enemies of the Aryans, and yogic practices are attested from the Indus civilization on.

Patron of the yogis, since he invented a method (*yoga*) which allows the virile force to be sublimated so as then to be transmuted into 'mental' energy through an internal alchemy and a subtle physiology, Shiva is the 'great yogi' (*mahayogin*). His erect member (*urdhvalinga*), sometimes represented in iconography, expresses the essential of chastity, since, according to the Mahabharata, the 'erect *linga* retains the seed while the lowered *linga* has discharged it'. Furthermore the Sanskrit term *urdhvaretas*, indicating the ejaculation of seed, also denotes the exercise of continence. So we can understand that the *lingas* of the Shivaite sanctuaries which figure an erect phallus are so many 'pillars of chastity'.

Classical iconography usually represents the Shiva yogi as an ascetic with a naked body covered in cinders (*vibhuti*); in the middle of his forehead is his third eye, called the 'eye of knowledge' (*jnananetra*), which consumed the body of the adventurous Kama, god of desire. The erect phallus of Shiva symbolizes his perfect mastery of the vital forces (*tapas*) and of desire. It is the vivid expression of the belief that love and death, ecstasy and asceticism, are fundamentally connected.

2. The speculative framework

The religious transformations brought about in the course of the 'Hindu synthesis', of which the renewal of the pantheon and the emergence of the great deities Vishnu and Shiva is one of the most visible consequences, equally affected the speculative framework around which religious reflection developed. This had to adapt to the new facts of rising Hinduism. In order to take account of the borrowings from the Vedic sources and the Hindu innovations, some of the main ideas of Hinduism were developed, particularly those about cosmogony, the structure of the universe and the world ages (*yugas*), the soul, the other world and deliverance (*moksha*).

If with the Rig Veda Vedism developed several scenarios to explain the origin of the world, the cosmogonic speculations of Hinduism, based on Samkhya philosophy, summed up this question by explaining the origin and formation of the universe from the evolution (*parinama*) of an original substratum, fundamental nature (*mula prakrti* or *prakrti*), which had existed from all eternity.

When original nature was still in an undeveloped

state, the three *gunas* were in equilibrium. But at a certain moment, as the result of the proximity of a spiritual monad (*purusha*), *prakrti* set in motion a long process of evolution, and the equilibrium between the three *gunas* was broken. At the end of this process of interaction, which simultaneously gave rise to phenomenal reality and the phenomena of the senses, the 'five coarse elements' (*pancabhutas*) or 'gross elements' (*mahabhutas*) came into being: space and ether (*akasha*), air, fire, water and earth, constituting the 'egg of Brahma' (*brahmanda*), i.e. the universe. From this cosmic egg was born Brahma, who engendered the creation. This was either through seven or ten Prajapatis (literally 'lords of creatures') as intermediaries, who gave birth to creatures, or by dividing himself into two poles, male and female. If the world can unfold itself through the evolution of an original substratum, Indian thought also conceived that this universe could dissolve itself, thus formulating for the first time the theory of the ages of the world.

The *brahmanda* is composed of two halves separated by the earth. The upper half comprises seven heavenly stages, of which the highest is the abode of *brahman*. The lower part, subdivided into seven subterranean stages (*patalas*), is the domain of the *nagas* and a quantity of fabulous beings. It is at the lowest base of the *patalas* that hell (*naraka*) is situated.

The earth, located between the two halves of the cosmic egg, has the form of a disc. In its midst rises the mythical Mount Meru, the real axis of the world around which the constellations gravitate. There are two theories about the disposition of the continents The first affirms that four islands (*dvipas*) are disposed around Mount Meru and that the island inhabited by humanity (*manusyaloka*) is situated in the south; it is called the 'isle of the rose apple' (*jambu dvipa*), a name also given to the continent of India. The second theory claims that the island of the rose apple extends around Mount Meru and that it is encircled by seven concentric continents separated by seven seas.

There are no Vedic antecedents to the Indian doctrine of the ages of the world. While the other classical civilizations envisaged human history in cycles of thousands or tens of thousands of years, Hindu tradition integrated human history and human life into a complex system of giant concentric cosmic cycles moving together but in a retrograde direction, the largest cycle corresponding to the total deployment of the possibilities of a world from its emanation (*srishti*) to its extinction, which comes about by a dissolution (*pralaya*). This doctrine begins to become structured at the beginning of the Hindu period and is developed in the epic literature, the Puranas and the Dharma Shastras. Thus in the famous Laws of Manu (end of Book 1, vv. 68–86), it is the object of an account linked to the story of successive creations following the great original creation.

According to Indian conceptions, the cycle of creations and destructions of the universe goes on *ad infinitum*. Each world cycle or cosmic era (*kalpa*), which is equivalent to a day in the life of Brahma, comprises one thousand *maha yugas* (literally 'great ages') divided each into four phases (*yugas*, literally 'ages') of increasingly shorter duration. These follow a decreasing arithmetical progression reflecting in the temporal order the progressive deterioration of the moral order (*dharma*). These four phases, named after throws of Indian dice, are respectively called *krita yuga* (literally age accomplished), *treta yuga* (literally age of the triad), *dvapara yuga* (literally age characterized by two) and *kali yuga* (literally evil age). They correspond to the ages in the Graeco–Roman tradition named after metals (ages of gold, silver, copper and iron, see Hesiod, *Works and Days*, 106–201).

The Hindu *krita yuga* is a golden age equivalent to the primordial periods of paradise in other traditions, during which the moral order is perfect and penetrates everything. Men know neither evils nor illnesses; they live for a long time and obtain the fulfilment of their desires, while justice and harmony reign on earth: 'truth reigns, and no good obtained by mortals derives from iniquity' (*Laws of Manu* I, 81). In the *treta yuga* there is already no more than three-quarters of the original *dharma*. It is in the course or this second age that the first evils appear and human life begins to decrease. During the *dvapara yuga* only half of *dharma* exists: evils get worse and the duration of human life decreases still further. In the *kali yuga*, the *dharma* is only a quarter of what it was during the *krita* age, and it is for this reason that this age is the worst of all: during it the values of truth and justice are scorned and moral degradation is at its height. In the present cycle, according to traditional calculations, the *kali yuga* has lasted for more than five thousand years, since it is thought to have begun with the death of Lord Krishna in 3102 BCE. The present *kali yuga* will come to an end when the avatar Kalki is manifested; he will usher in a new golden age, the coming of which will be preceded by a cosmic dissolution.

According to the facts given in the Laws of Manu (I, 69ff.), each age (*yuga*) of a *maha yuga* is preceded by a dawn and followed by a twilight equivalent to a tenth of the duration of the said age. A *maha yuga* lasts for 12,000 divine years (*Laws of Manu* I, 71). Consequently, the four ages which constitute it last respectively (taking account of the arithmetical decrease and adding the duration of their dawn and twilight): 4,000 + (2 x 400) = 4,800 years for the *krita yuga*; 3,000 + (2 x 300) = 3,600 years for the *treta yuga*; 2,400 years for the *dvapara yuga*; and 1,200 for the *kali yuga*. As a divine year corresponds to 3,609 years of human life, the duration of the four ages expressed in human years is 1,728,000 for the *krita yuga*, 1,296,000 for the *treta yuga*, 864,000 for the *dvapara yuga*, and 432,000 for the *kali yuga*, which gives a total duration of 4,320,000 human years for the *maha yuga*. Since 1,000 *maha yugas* constitute one day in the life of Brahma (one night of Brahma being the same duration), and since his life is 100 divine years, we end up at the fantastic number of 311,040 billion human years for the total duration of the whole of the external cycle, which will end in the 'great dissolution' (*mahapralaya*), in the course of which everything will disappear and return to *prakrti*. In mythical mode, only the primordial waters will remain, with the Lord Vishnu sleeping on their surface, lying on the coils of the serpent Sesha.

Hindu tradition has similarly divided the *kalpas* into fourteen *manvantaras* (*manu* + *atara* = *manvantara*, literally intervals between the Manu), each comprising 71 *maha yugas*. The name *manvantara* comes from Manu, the Noah of Indian mythology, since each cycle is thought to end with a dissolution which takes the form of a deluge. According to traditional calculations we are now in the seventh *manvantara* ruled by the Manu Vaivasvata, the six former ones constituting the past *manvantaras* and the seven subsequent ones the future *manvantara*. So as to make the two systems coincide, it is supposed that the first *manvantara* of each *kalpa* was preceded by a long dawn of a *krita yuga* and that each *manvantara* was followed by a twilight of the same length. That establishes the equivalence between *manvantara* and *mahayuga*: 1 *kalpa* = (14 x 71) = (0.4 x 15) or 994 + 6 = 1,000 *maha yugas*.

At the end of the Vedic age, speculations on survival are profoundly renewed by the Upanishads. Up to that point, as we have had the occasion to note, in essential there were two views of life after death. On the one hand the dead person was thought to remain near his house in a larval existence in a subterranean abyss; on the other, through the flame and smoke of the funeral pyre he ascended to heaven where, having recovered his body, he spent pleasant days in a paradise (*svarga*) in the company of the gods.

Furthermore the Vedic texts contrasted two 'ways' (*yanas*): that of the gods, which they take when they come to be present at sacrifices, and that of the spirits of the dead, which leads to a subterranean world, a way which is taken by the 'fathers' (*pitr*) when they come back to earth to consume the sacrifices prepared by their descendants for them. When it was accepted that certain mortals could attain heaven, the system needed certain changes. The doctrine of the transmigration of souls (*samsara*) begun by the Upanishad literature made it possible to resolve this contradiction.

Handed down in the earliest Upanishads and also by Buddhist sources, two new interdependent concepts – those of *karma* (literally 'act') and *samsara* (literally current) progressively emerged from the eighth to sixth centuries BCE and eventually formed the two poles around which all Hindu eschatology was constructed. Despite hypotheses formulated in an attempt to explain their origin (referring to cyclical thought and doubt about the efficacy of ritual, and also aboriginal borrowing), we have to recognize that as yet there is still no satisfactory answer to this question. However, it is worth noting that the period during which these two notions appeared coincides with the development of speculations on the mechanisms of psychology and the relationship between the body and the spirit and the self (*atman*).

At any rate, before looking at the meaning of the concepts of *karma* and *samsara*, it is worth considering the way in which the relationship between body and soul was conceived of in ancient India.

Because they had no precise and complex terminology, Hindu doctrines do not seem to have identified a principle corresponding precisely to the Western notion of the soul, so that the content of various Indian words (*atman, purusha, jiva*) is more extensive than our notion of soul. It denotes knowledge with the will and even the sensations. Perhaps *jiva* or *jivatman* comes closest to the notion of individual soul, since it represents *atman* itself as present in the body, ruling over it, preserving and guiding it. *Atman* in the chain of successive existences (*samsara*) is what assures the unity of the individual destiny.

Furthermore, it needs to be emphasized that Hinduism does not separate the soul and body in such a radical way, since it sees a continuity between the bodily world and psychological principles. Alongside the visible body made up of the seven organic constituents (bone, marrow, blood, etc.), which is linked with psychological processes by 'breaths' (*pranas*), the texts describe the existence of another body, invisible and transcendent, called the 'subtle body'. This latter serves to some degree to support the psychological apparatus: it comprises the subtle sense organs and the internal organ which controls the totality of psychological processes (the senses, the ego-sense and the discriminative faculty). On physical death the soul leaves the body by one of the nine bodily openings, accompanied by the 'subtle body', which takes with it information about the individual future inscribed on the *karma*.

In Vedism, the term *karma* denotes the sacrifice (*yajna*), i.e. the ritual 'act' *par excellence* which on the one hand allows the social and cosmic order (*dharma*) to maintain itself and on the other assures the person sacrificing an immortality in the other world.

This immortality procured by the merits (*punyas*) of the rite does not seem to have been felt to be definitive, since the texts show that Vedic man was afraid of suffering *punar-mrtyu* (literally 're-death' or 'recurrent death') in the beyond once the merits accumulated by the practice of ritual had been exhausted. Under the joint influence of the literature of the Upanishads and the current of ascetics (*samnyasin*) affirming that man must free himself from this re-death, the term *karma* came to be applied to just or unjust actions, i.e. actions in conformity with or in contradiction to the social and cosmic order (*dharma*). The basic idea is that in addition to its immediate and visible effect, the act has a subtle and transcendent effect ultimately capable of guiding human destiny. That changed eschatology as follows. A just action engenders a merit (*punya*), which will later be the source of joys, while conversely an unjust action engenders a demerit (*papman*) which, sooner or later, will bring pain and suffering. This doctrine is summed up admirably by the Brihadaranyaka Upanishad (III, 2, 13), which explains that one becomes good by a good action and bad by a bad action. Another ancient Upanishad, the Chandogya Upanishad (V, 10, 1–10), lays down three possible destinies for souls. The first concerns 'those who know thus'. They rejoin *brahman* by the way of the gods and are fused with it. Those among them who are con-

What is Vedanta?

Vedanta is the most famous and most prestigious of the six philosophical systems (*darshanas*) recognized by Brahminic orthodoxy. Initially its function seems to have been complementary to Mimamsa, namely to produce an exegesis of the non-ritualistic, i.e. speculative or 'mystical', portions of the Vedas. These portions to a very great extent correspond with the Upanishads, which are rightly also called Vedantas (in the plural). They represent revealed truth (*sruti*), while the Bhagavad Gita incarnates the 'authorized tradition' (*smrti*). Furthermore, like all *darshanas*, the Vedanta is composed on the basis of a collection of aphorisms, the Vedanta Sutras or Brahma Sutras attributed to the sage Badarayana (third century BCE?). So the system has a threefold point of departure (*prasthanatraya*).

However, it should be realized that 'Vedanta' is far more a generic term than the designation of a precise philosophical doctrine. The reason is, quite simply, that the texts of the Upanishads, which are often obscure and contradictory, and even more the Brahma Sutras, because of their extreme conciseness, have given rise to a mass of differing interpretations. Furthermore, the 'prehistory' of the Vedanta is utterly inaccessable to us: more than ten centuries elapsed between the redaction of the Sutras and the first extant commentary, that of Sankara.

In practice, five lines of interpretation have been retained by the tradition, each one deriving from the work of one of the 'great' commentators on the Sutras. These are, in chronological order of their appearance:

1. Non-dualist Vedanta (*Advaita Vedanta*), founded by Sankara in the eighth century;
2. The 'non-dualism of the differenced' (*Visistadvaita*), which goes back to Ramanuja (eleventh to twelfth centuries);
3. The 'dualist and non-dualist' doctrine (*Bhedabheda*) proposed by Nimbarka in the thirteenth century;
4. The 'dualism' (*dvaita*) of Madhava (thirteenth century);
5. The 'pure non-dualism' (*Suddhadvaita*) which emerges from the work of Vallabha (fifteenth-sixteenth century).

The common denominator of all these doctrines can be reduced to a few elements, apart from the obvious fact that they all recognize the authority of the Upanishads and the Bhagavad Gita. Certainly, the main theme of some of them is *brahman* and the possibility of the individual self (*atman*) being united with it in deliverance. Otherwise, they differ on everything.

So it is a misuse of language to speak in the singular of Vedantic doctrine, a term which is almost always used to denote the non-dualistic school founded by Sankara. This usage is explained in turn – without any justification – by the fact that the school of Sankara came out on top over the centuries. Not only did it benefit from being the earliest school, but the number and quality of its representatives – quite apart from its illustrious founder – assured that its influence would spread all over India, indeed all over the world, down to the present day, while its rivals were restricted to a provincial and 'sectarian' audience.

(Michel Hulin, 'Vedanta' in
Les Notions Philosophiques 2, 2924)

---

formed to the demands of religion obtain the right to rebirth, but this rebirth is directly linked to the state of their *karma*: 'those who have a satisfactory conduct have the prospect of obtaining a satisfactory birth, Brahmin, Kshatriya or Vaishya. Those, by contrast, who are stained by bad conduct have the prospect of a soiled birth, as dog, pig or Candala [without a caste]' (V, 10, 7). A third way relates to the lower forms of life which have no moral sanctions (insects, worms, etc.). The destiny of

The Laws of Manu

A man experiences in his mind and heart the good or bad effects of past actions committed in his mind and heart, in his speech what he has committed in his speech, and in his body what he has committed with his body. A man becomes a stationary object as a result of the faults that are the effects of past actions of the body, a bird or wild animal from those of speech, and a member of one of the lowest castes from those of the mind and heart . . .

Now I will tell you, in a nutshell and in order, the transmigrations in this whole universe that one achieves by each quality. People of lucidity become gods, people of energy become humans, and people of darkness always become animals; this is the three-fold level of existence. But it should be realized that this three-fold level of existence, which is dependent on the qualities, is itself threefold: lowest, middle and highest, according to the specific act and learning (of the actor).

Stationary objects, worms and bugs, fish, snakes, turtles, livestock, and wild animals are the hindmost level of existence to which darkness leads. Elephants, horses, servants, despised barbarians, lions, tigers and boars are the middle level of existence to which darkness leads. Strolling actors, birds, deceiving men, ogres and ghouls are the highest level of existence to which darkness leads . . .

Ascetics, renouncers, priests, the hosts of gods who fly about on celestial chariots, the constellations and the anti-gods are the first level of existence to which lucidity leads. Sacrificers, sages, gods, the Vedas, the celestial lights, the years, the ancestors and the Amenables are the second level of existence to which lucidity leads. Wise men say that Brahma, the creator of the whole universe, religion, the great one, and the unmanifest are the highest level of existence to which lucidity leads.

All that results from the three sorts of action that has thus been explained, the entire system of transmigration for all living beings, which is divided into three types, each of which is further subdivided into three.

(XII, 8–9, 39–50)

---

those creatures who do not produce *karma* is subject to a single decree: their condition is to be born and to die.

This idea of the maturation of the act takes place exclusively in the organ which was the origin of this act. This is what is said in the Laws of Manu.

By its quasi-mechanical functioning, the law of *karma* seems to make each individual responsible, since it is only by the infinite cycle of rebirths (*samsara*) that one becomes the good or evil that one has merited. However, *karma* and the play of merits and demerits should not be imagined as a bank account with a credit or a debit balance. In fact the law of *karma* is distributive. It is a retribution which requires a great deal of time, and this means that essentially it has no beginning or end, since the present situation of a being is already the result of the weight of that being's past actions (*sancita karma*).

It is at this stage that we have a better understanding of the idea of universal transmigration (*samsara*). The *samsara* which serves to some degree as 'support' for the *karma* in fact extends to all phenomena, including minerals, plants and animals, but also the world of the gods, genies and demons. In the intermediate zone it also extends to the human condition. The human condition seems the most privileged of all, since it is the only state in which good or bad *karma* can be accumulated by voluntary action. So we can understand the human condition as the only one which allows the person in it to be able to compel 'his' destiny and influence

The Idea of 'Reincarnation' for Non-Hindus

The *karma* theory tells us that we have lived lives that we cannot remember and hence cannot feel. But for those of us who lack the imagination to perceive the infinity of our lives in time, it might be possible to perceive the infinity of our lives in human space. Again, the Indian texts tell us that we are karmically linked to all the other people in the world; *they are us*. I have known and respected this theory for a long time, though I have not always believed it. But for one important moment, I did believe it. It was at a time when I was feeling rather sorry for myself for having only one child; I wished that I had had lots of children, and now it was too late. I felt that having six children would have meant having an entirely different life, not merely six times the life of a woman with one child, and I wanted that life as well as the life that I had. This thought was in my mind as I wandered on a beach in Ireland, and saw a women with lots and lots of children, very nice children, too, and at their best, as young children often are on a beach. Normally, I would have envied her; but this time, I enjoyed her children. I was happy to watch them. And suddenly I felt that they were mine, that the woman on the beach had had them for me, so that they would be there for me to watch them as they played in the water. Her life was my life too; I felt it then, and I remember it now. What had been an idea to me until then, the idea of my karmic identity with other people, became an experience. I was able to live her life in my imagination.

One way of interpreting my epiphany of the woman on the beach was this realization that my connection to her – and, through her, to every other woman who had ever had or ever would have children – meant that my brief life-span was expanded into the life-spans of all the other people in the world. This is a very Hindu way of looking at one's relationship with all other people. Woven through the series of individual lives, each consisting of a cluster of experiences, was the thread of the experience itself – in this case, motherhood. That experience would survive when her children and mine were long dead.

I felt then that all the things that one wanted to do and to be existed in eternity; they stood there for ever, as long as there was human life on the planet Earth. They were like beautiful rooms that anyone could walk into; and when I could no longer walk into them, they would still be there. They were part of time, and though they could not go on being part of me for much longer, part of me would always be there in them. Something of me would still linger on in those things that I had loved, like the perfume or pipe smoke that tells you that someone else has been in a room before you. This is the same 'perfume', the same karmic trace of memory, that adheres to the transmigrating soul. And through my connection with the woman on the beach, I would be the people in the future who sensed in that room the perfume that it had left behind, though (unless I was a gifted sage), I would not recognize it as my perfume. Perhaps, since I am not a Hindu, that is as close as I can come to believing that I can remember my other lives: remembering other peoples' lives as my life. And perhaps it is close enough.

(Wendy Doniger, 'Reincarnation in Hinduism', *Concilium* 1993/5, 13f.)

---

it in one direction or another. That might appear surprising, but it is also explained that the divine condition no longer really allows this choice since, in their everyday life of paradise, the gods increasingly get into a kind of indolence in which each day they exhaust more of the merits that they had previously accumulated. At the bottom of the scale of beings, the 'inferior' beings are too dull and brutalized by the torpor into which their state plunges them to produce *karma* since, being stripped of moral sanctions, they cannot distinguish right actions from wrong actions.

Thus despite what is often heard in the West, *karma* is the very opposite of a fatalistic doctrine, since it invites an interpretation of the human condition as a precious opportunity offered to people to influence the course of their destinies.

However, the ultimate aim is not rebirth but the completion of the cycle of rebirths to obtain deliverance (*moksha*). Deliverance can be attained in several ways. In the theistic currents of *bhakti* and Tantrism, deliverance does not necessitate the renunciation of society (see the Bhagavad Gita), but this is rejected by systems like non-dualistic Vedanta, Samkhya and the classical Yogas. Furthermore, in the theistic currents it is the grace (*prasada*) of the deity in which the *bhakta* abandons himself that confers liberating knowledge on him, whereas elsewhere (in Samkhya, for example) the disciple can count only on himself and the help of his master (*guru*). In the same way, the state of the one who is delivered is thought of differently, depending on the school. In the *bhakti* tendencies, those who are delivered keep their individual personalities. They are not fused in the deity, but perpetually enjoy his presence in unity with him. By contrast, in currents like non-dualistic Vedanta, deliverance is linked to the dissolution of the individual personality and is then fusion with *brahman*.

3. Hindu rites and festivals

According to the law of *karma*, human activity affects one's future condition and is to some degree a creator of one's destiny. To conform in all things to the socio-cosmic order (*dharma*), i.e. at the individual level to observe one's own *dharma* (*svadharma*) corresponding to one's present condition (age, status, etc.) and the demands of one's caste, to practise pious works (fasts, pilgrimages), allows the accumulation of merits (*punyas*) but does not provide direct orientation on the way to deliverance (*moksha*). Similarly, rites allow one to direct one's life on the good way, but are not enough to stop the wheel of *samsara*. They satisfy the needs of the religious and the piety of the masses, since it is evident that the one who renounces (*sannyasi*), the hermit or itinerant cut off from family and social life, who focusses his life solely on the quest for deliverance by exploring ascetic ways in order to attain the state of the 'living delivered one' (*jivan-mukta*) in this life, concerns a spiritual elite which represents only a tiny proportion of believers.

However, thanks to the network of ashrams in which gurus live, most of them having renounced the world, disciples engaged in the world can join them and follow their teachings. Furthermore, these privileged places of retreat contribute largely towards maintaining the idea of deliverance among individuals living in the world. They are also the only link which allow a non-Hindu to be integrated into Hinduism, since Hinduism excludes conversion (one is a Hindu by birth); through them one can renounce the world like one's master and thus become his disciple.

To simplify things, one could divide Hindu rites into three main groups. First there are everyday private rites, usually performed at home by a householder who is 'twice born'. To these everyday practices are added ceremonies connected with the cycle of initiation and rites of passage (*samskara*) beginning from before the birth of any 'twice born', through a serious of pre-natal rites performed over the future mother, and culminating for boys with the ceremony of initiation (*upanayana*) and for girls with marriage, ending for both sexes on the funeral pyre of the dead person, which closes the cycle of his or her life. Finally, there are the rites of the cycle of religious festivals, some celebrated all over India, others limited to certain regions. All are organized from different traditional lunar-solar calendars still in use on the sub-continent.

The everyday devotions of the orthodox Hindu are

generally made near to the family altar in the house, which is sometimes put in a small room that has been specially furnished. Often modest, this altar will primarily contain the statue or rather the 'image' (*pratima*) of the chosen deity (*ishta devata*) revered by the family tradition, and the images of other gods, to which are added several utensils needed for private worship (an oil lamp, joss sticks, incense, consecrated ash, wood and plates with the offerings: flowers, fruit and cakes). Here it is possible only to give a very general survey of the everyday rites, without taking account of the many variants linked to the 'sects' (*sampradaya*) and regional specialisms.

The morning rites (*pratah samhdya*) begin before sunrise. They include, first, cleaning the teeth and a series of external ablutions in the form of a shower or a bath, followed by internal ablutions which consist of purifying the mouth several times with water taken in the palm of the hand. This is *achamana*.

The moment the sun rises over the horizon, the faithful 'twice born' or the orthodox Brahmin recites several times the famous *savitri*, praise to the sun (*surya*) in its aspect as generator (*savirtr*), which originates from a verse of the Rig Veda (III, 62, 10) and which every 'twice born' learns on the day of his initiation (*upanayana*) after being invested with the sacred thread:

'May we possess this desirable ray of the God Savitr, so that it prompts our thoughts.'

This recitation, which coincides with the rising of the sun, corresponds precisely to the junction (*sandhya*) of day and night; it is thought to deliver the sun from the hand of the demons. It is repeated in the evening at twilight. According to the *Laws of Manu* (II, 101–102), the daily recitation of the *savitri* obliterates sins. The dawn recitation effaces sins committed during the night and the evening recitation effaces those of the day.

This important rite can be supplemented (particularly among the Brahmins) by other devotions, like the recitation of certain words (*mantras*) or the reading of a passage taken from the scriptures (*brahmayajna*) and a silent meditation accompanied by breathing exercises (*pranayama*) or even a murmured recitation (*japa*).

The basic rite, performed every day by the master of the house, sometimes helped by his bride or celebrated by the domestic Brahmin employed by the great families, is called *puja* (root *puj*, literally honour). It consists in veneration of the image of the deity which the family tradition has chosen to honour. This icon is the heart of the family altar. It is always made according to rigorous criteria intended to limit as far as possible the escapades of human imagination and fantasy.

In the mind of the faithful, this material image (which is sometimes a statue) is neither a simple representation of the god nor even a religious symbol thought to represent that god. For the believer, this cultic image (*murti*, root *murch*, literally 'solidify') crystallizes, or rather concentrates, the divine presence which is so to speak projected. The image, far from being the reflection of the deity, is more the vehicle of a real archetypal presence. As an imprint of the divine archetype, the divine image is thus the place where the deity shows himself, where his face, whether human or animal, appears without a veil and is turned to each person according to his capacity to receive it. So veneration of the image should not be described as idolatry, since if this image is correctly made, it is to some degree consubstantial with what it represents. The veneration shown to it in fact goes back to the divine prototype.

The *puja* is primarily homage shown to the chosen deity and then to the other gods, a homage patterned on the Indian rites of hospitality. In Hinduism, this ritual is the equivalent of the 'sacrifice' (*yajna*) of Vedic times. It has been substituted for the complex and expensive, sometimes bloody, sacrifices of Vedism, apparently under the influence in Brahminic India of the notion of *ahimsa* (literally 'no-harming'), handed down by Buddhism and Jainism.

Traditionally, a *puja* comprises sixteen 'actions'

India and the Cult of the Cow

What underlies the Indian veneration of the cow? It has a long and complex history. Suppose we go back to the Veda. The Aryans, the people who invaded the north-west of the Indian sub-continent from the west in the course of the ten to fifteen centuries before the Christian eras, were both pastoral and warlike. In the Vedic hymns which they composed there and throughout the Vedic literature there is frequent mention of herds of cattle, because they were sacrificial animals and the great spoil in war. The cow was appreciated by these peoples not only for its economic value (in terms of both milk and meat) but also for its ritual function, which was indispensable to Vedic sacrifice. Animal sacrifice was the central element of Vedic religion. The Veda does not know the doctrine of *ahimsa* (not harming), which was put forward only around the sixth century BCE by Mahavira, the Jain, and Siddhartha Gautama, the Buddha, and then progressively accepted by renunciants, by high-caste Hindus and finally by the masses. To kill for sacrifice was not to kill, and to eat sacrificial meat was allowed. So it is not surprising to discover that the cow is on the list of five victims worthy to be sacrificed at the solemn Vedic sacrifices, or that the officiating Brahmin priests and the one offering the sacrifice ate the flesh of this animal after it had been sacrificed.

Similarly, the products of the cow (butter, whey, cream, cheese) constituted the ritual offering called *ida*. Furthermore, the celebration of the Vedic sacrifice called for an assembly of officiating Brahmin priests to whom the one offering the sacrifice had to pay a 'ritual salary' (*daksina*) aimed at his ascension to heaven. The offering of one or more cows was one of the four kinds of payment recognized. Moreover, this tradition has remained alive in Hindu India.

To return to the Veda. Why is the cow sacred? The Rig Veda regards the Brahmin's cow as equal to the Aditi, equal to the earth. Now the Brahmin, a god among men, the one who has the Vedic word, contributes (in association with the king) to the maintenance of the cosmic and socio-religious order (*dharma*). To protect the order of the world it is necessary to protect the Brahmin's cow. From an economic and religious perspective, the veneration of the milk-cow is quite understandable, as are the sacred character and inviolability of the cow or cows belonging to the Brahmins. Even today, when a Hindu comes across a particularly superb specimen, with the tips of its horns gilded, its forehead painted vermilion, and garlands round its neck, he will involuntarily exclaim, 'That's more than a cow, that's a deity (*devata*)!'

For all these reasons, which relate as much to the heart as the reason, Gandhi said: 'For me, the cow represents the totality of the sub-human world. Through it, human beings are made aware of their identity with all living things. To protect the cow is to protect all in the divine creation which is not endowed with the word.' This helps us to understand better why, when the harvest is late and the farmer has to leave his land burned by the sun to take refuge in the suburbs, he treats his cow as a member of the family and takes it with him. He has an implicit contract with it. We might say that in India the cow is a domestic animal. And just as a Westerner would never dream of eating a dog or cat, it would be impiety for a Hindu to eat a cow.

(Lakshmi Kapani, 'L'hindouisme', in Jean Delumeau, *Le fait religieux*, 381–4).

(*upacaras*); in other words, it is composed of sixteen successive rites accompanied by songs and mantras. However, in the domestic *puja* the number of these rites is often fewer, and the ceremony consists essentially in lighting an oil lamp on the altar, making offerings of flowers, and saying a prayer which includes the recitation of *mantras*.

The important elements of a more elaborate *puja*, not taking into account variants linked to the cult of the different 'sects', are as follows: purification of the celebrant (*achamana*), invocation of the deity (*avahana*), offering of water and rice (*arghya*), consecration of the image by the aspersion of water (*abhiseka*), dressing and perfuming the icon (*vastropavita*), offering flowers (*puspanjali*), offering incense and light (*dhupadipa*), oblation by fire (*homa*), offering of food (*naivedya*), concluding rites (*udvasana*).

In addition to the domestic *puja*, there are also the *pujas* celebrated in the temples and the annual collective *pujas* which in certain cities attract a considerable number of pilgrims.

While the *pujas* are post-Vedic, the rites connected with the unfolding of the life-cycle (*samskaras*) by contrast go back to Vedic times. They concern the individuals of the first three *varnas*, those who are described as 'twice-born' (*dvija*). As we have seen, the *samskaras* are both purificatory rites aimed at washing away the biological impurity of birth and rites of perfection. The most important are still celebrated today in orthodox families. They are *garbhadhana*, a pre-natal rite aimed at ensuring conception, rites relating to birth (*jatakarma*), *annaprasana* (a rite of weaning), *cudakarana* (first cutting of the hair), marriage (*vivaha*) and funerary rites (*antyesti*). By contrast, *upanayana* (initiation of a young boy by a Brahmanic master) has been emptied of some of its significance because teaching has become more general; however, its religious impact remains important.

Alongside the everyday religious practice of the family in the house or the temple, the religious festivals also form an important moment in the life of every Hindu. These festivals are so numerous, given the different tendencies which make up Hinduism, that one can rightly say that there is never a day in India on which a festival is not celebrated.

If the states constituting the Indian union officially use the Gregorian calendar for civic matters, the traditional calendars of a lunar-solar type are the background to the religious festivals. Before mentioning the organization of the calendar, it should be explained that in addition to the Buddhist and Muslim eras observed in the two communities, there are other eras by which the years can be dated, notably the Vikrama era (*Vikramakala*) which begins in 58 BCE and is still largely used in central and western India, and the Shaka era (*Shakakala*), which began in 78 CE and is used by the vast majority of the country.

The different calendars which India has used in the course of its history take into account the phases of the moon and the apparent movements of the sun (the shift in the zodiacal constellations). That is why they are called lunar-solar. However, because of the shorter duration of the lunar year (around 354 days) by comparison with the solar year (around 365 and one quarter days), the Indian astronomers had to work out a system making it possible to re-establish a concordance between the two years by the regular addition of an embolismic month called *adhika masa* (literally additional month), to avoid the lunar months wandering through the seasons.

The names of the twelve lunar months come from the names of twelve of the twenty-eight 'lunar mansions' (*naksatra*) thought to accompany the moon during a complete cycle of twelve full moons. Each lunar month (*chandramasa*) is divided into two fortnights (*paksa*, literally 'wing'). The first, called 'bright' (*sukla paksa*), begins with the new moon and ends with the full moon, the period during which the moon 'grows' and thus becomes brighter; the second, called 'dark' (*krishna paksa*), begins on the day of the full moon and ends with the next new moon, i.e. during the period in which the moon 'decreases'.

Depending on the geographical location and the era used, the lunar month begins either with the new moon or the full moon. The lunar-solar year

The Hindu Calendar

Lunar-Solar Month	Name	Gregorian Equivalent	Associated Deity
I	Chaitra	March–April	Nirriti
II	Vaishakh	April–May	Vayu
III	Jyaishtha	May–June	Agni
IV	Ashard	June–July	Sanmukha
V	Shravan	July–August	Samudra
VI	Bhadra	August–September	Ganesha
VII	Ashvin	September–October	Sakra
VIII	Kartik	October–November	Brahma
IX	Agrahayan	November–December	Rudra
X	Paush	December–January	Kubera
XI	Magh	January–February	Vishnu
XII	Phalgun	February–March	Yama

begins at the spring equinox (around 21 March), usually with the month of Chaitra (21 March–20 April) or that of Vaisakh.

A deity is associated with each month. All the information is listed in the box above.

Problems associated with local variants and the fact that the same deity (Shiva, Vishnu) can be venerated under different names, depending on the region, further complicated by the fixing of the date of the beginning of the year, mean that it is impossible to mention all the religious festivals of the Hindu calendar or even the most important ones. So here is a representative survey of the main festivals today, with some indication of the relationship between them and other earlier festivals.

The month of Chaitra is essentially marked by two types of festival, on the one hand rejoicing over the new year which is the occasion for family gatherings, and on the other the celebration of the birth of Rama (seventh avatar). This festival, called Ramanavami, is celebrated on the ninth day of the bright fortnight of the month. It commemorates the action of Rama, whose story the Ramayana relates, and is celebrated with exceptional intensity in the Vishnuite temples of the country, but more particularly in the state of Uttar Pradesh, notably at Ayodhya, the city in which Rama was born. It then became his capital, where he reigned as a model and enlightened prince. Another festival, Hanuman Jayanti, celebrated on the day of the full moon of Chaitra, is a feast of Hanuman, the leader of the monkeys and companion of Rama.

Two other avatars of Vishnu are celebrated during the following month (Vaisakh). The third day of the bright fortnight is dedicated to Parasurama (sixth avatar), particularly venerated in the central and western region of the country, and ten days later there is a more special celebration of the man-lion (Narasimha) in Andhra Pradesh.

In the same month, the festival of Vaishakh opens the Hindu solar year. Within the Sikh community, this festival commemorates the creation of the Khalsa (a Sikh martial order) by Guru Gobind Singh in 1699.

The month of Jyaishtha is not marked by any important festivals.

In the month of Ashard the Brahmanic schools and the ashrams celebrate the festival of the spiritual masters, which pays homage both to Vyasa, the mythical compiler of the Veda (Vedavyasa) and the supposed author of the Mahabharata, and to the spiritual master (*guru*) who conferred initiation (*upanayana*) on the male children of the family. In the case of the latter, the cult is not addressed to the man, but to the deity thought to live in him and of whom he is the living incarnation.

Traditionally, according to the Hindu calendar, the disciples of a master venerate him every week on Thursdays; this is called *guruvara* or *guruvasara*, i.e. the day of the masters.

During the same month, at Puri (in the state of Orissa), one of the most spectacular festivals in the Hindu calendar is held. In the presence of a great crowd of faithful there is a celebration of Vishnu Jagannath ('protector of the world'), who has been assimilated to Krishna. This takes the form of a procession of chariots (*raths*). The faithful jostle to draw the three monumental chariots in the form of temples (this is a meritorious act) in which have been put the statues of Jagannath, his brother Balabhadra and his sister Subhadra.

On the fifth day of the bright fortnight of the month of Shravan, India honours snakes (*nagas*) and more particularly cobras. Celebrated with great verve at Jodhpur (in the state of Rajasthan), a city in which there are great effigies of *nagas* on homes and temples, Nag Panchami is above all a festival for the women, who offer milk and other gifts to the votive cobras of the temples. On this day no work is done on the land. Several episodes of mythology introduce the serpents. Here attention should be drawn to the importance in the collective Hindu unconscious of the mythical snake with a thousand heads called Ananta or Sesha, which floats on the surface of the waters between two cosmic eras (*kalpas*), and on which Vishu rests. In the same way, all the faithful of Krishna know the famous episode told by the Harivansa (chs. LV and LVI) in which the child Krishna fights and tames the five-headed serpent Kaliya on the banks of the Yamuna.

In the north and west of the country, on the day of the full moon of the month of Shravan, the young girls have a custom of putting bracelets of silk or cord (*rahkis*) on the wrists of their brothers; these are thought to protect them from evil fates. This festival, which is aimed at strengthening fraternal bonds, is called *rahki bandhan* in Hindi and in Sanskrit *raksaban-hapurmima*, i.e. 'the festival of the full moon when the amulets (*raksa*) are attached'.

In the month of Bhadra, on the eighth day of the dark fortnight, Vishnuite India celebrates the birth of Krishna. This feast called Krishnajanmastami is celebrated with exceptional fervour at Mathura and Vrindaban (in the state of Uttar Pradesh), the city in which the god was born and the place in the forest where Krishna looked after the herds, which have become two holy cities of Krishnaism. The attractions at the festival include dances (*rasalila*) recalling the uninhibited dances which the god performed with the shepherdesses (*gopi*) and which have been popularized by Krishnaite iconography.

The same month, especially in Maharashtra, the birth of Ganesha, the popular god with the elephant head, is celebrated. His image or his statue are carried in procession and are then plunged into the sea or the rivers.

Around the same time (August–September), there is the festival of Onam, limited to the state of Kerala. For ten days there is a celebration both of the rice harvest and of the annual return of a local demon, the king of the *daityas* (a class of *asura*). This is Bali, conquered by Vishnu Vamana. During the festival of Onam, the houses are covered with floral decorations and the young people take part in the famous regattas of snake boats.

The month of Ashvin (September–October) begins with the 'nine nights' (*navaratri*) of the goddess; in other words, the first nine days of the month are consecrated to the goddesses Mahalakshmi, Mahakali and Mahasarasvati. However, under these three forms it is to Shakti and more particularly to Durga (literally 'the inaccessible') that homage is paid. This festival, which includes days of fasting, *pujas* and animal sacrifices, culminates on the tenth day (*dasahara* or *dussehra*, which is also called *vijaya dasami* literally 'victory of the tenth day'). On that day, in Bengal there is a commemoration of the victory of the goddess Durga over a demonic buffalo called Mahisha or Mahishasurta, and in other regions of the victory of Rama over the demon Ravana and his return to Ayodhya.

In October–November, in the month of Kartik, the festival of Dipavali or Divali is dedicated to Divali Mata, the 'mother of the festival of Divali'. This is none other than Lakshmi, goddess of abundance and happiness. For four to six days, little multicoloured lamps (*dipas*) are lit in the streets and houses and there are processions with fireworks including vast numbers of fire-crackers, which are thought to drive away the demons. This festival also marks the beginning of the financial year (settling of accounts).

In Tamil country, the festival of *pongal* (Tamil, literally 'boiling') is both a peasant harvest festival during which new rice (*navanna*) is offered as a first-fruit and a festival in honour of cattle, destined to ensure their prosperity for the coming year. For two days the married women prepare the mixture of new rice and sugared milk which gives the festival its name. This is offered to several deities, to all the persons present and to the cattle. In the Deccan and in the north of India, this festival, which is inserted into the month of Paush, around 12 January, is called *samkranti* (literally passage). It corresponds to the moment when the sun enters the zodiacal constellation of Capricorn and begins its northern course from the winter solstice. So it is a festival celebrating the rebirth of the sun. The difference between the present real date of the winter solstice (21–22 December) and the date of the celebration of this festival arises from the phenomenon of the precession of equinoxes.

The spring festival (*vasantapancami*) which takes place on the fifth day of the bright fortnight of the month of Magh is devoted to the goddess Sarasvati who, before being identified with Vach (goddess of the Word) in the Vedic period, was a god of rivers. Today Sarasvati is thought to be a manifestation of knowledge and study and the patroness of poetry and music. On this occasion it is the custom for students to present their books and work before the image of the deity and musicians their instruments so that she will help them in their creative activity.

Shiva Ratri (literally, the 'night of Shiva'), the fourteenth night of the dark fortnight of the month of Phalgun (February–March), is an all-night vigil celebrating the glory of Shiva in the course of which the *linga* is venerated. The passage about the appearance of the *linga* of fire to Brahma and Vishnu in the Linga Purana is the mythological basis for this festival.

Celebrated at the full moon of Phalgun, Holi is an ancient spring and fertility festival which has inherited another festival, the *madanotsava* (festival of Madana) dedicated to Kama, the god of love. In northern India, this festival is nowadays dedicated to Krishna, while in the south it commemorates the day when, with the help of the eye in his forehead, Shiva burned Kama, who had dared to disturb the asceticism of the great yogi.

Holi is also a kind of carnival, during which the order of the world is temporarily abolished. The most spectacular rite of the present festival, which probably goes back to the fertility rites of the ancient festival, is sprinkling passers-by with jets of coloured water from long syringes, a distant souvenir of the fertilizing water of *holi* which was once scattered.

To the calendar festivals other types of festival must be added. On the one hand there are the more or less local festivals which celebrate eminent saints or famous mystical poets or brahmanic doctors still engraved on people's memories, and on the other hand the *melas*, giant community festivals connected with certain astronomical constellations. At regular intervals and in certain places these bring together considerable crowds of pilgrims and faithful. The most famous of them, the Kumbh Melas, are connected with the planet Jupiter and its year, corresponding approximately to a cycle of twelve solar years. These Kumbh Melas also commemorate a mythical event which has been mentioned above, the 'churning of the ocean of milk' (*ksirodamathana*). It is related that having churned the sea of milk in the company of the gods, the Asuras succeeded in temporarily stealing a pot (*kumbha*) of ambrosia which came out of the waves. In their haste, they let some of the drops of divine nectar fall on the ground, which became eminently sacred. These geographical points correspond to the cites of Haridwar (state of Uttar Pradesh), Nashik (state of Maharashtra), Prayag, present-day Allahabad (state of Uttar Pradesh) and Ujjain (state of Madhya Pradesh). In them a Kumbh Mela is organized alternately every three years.

These holy cities, to which should be added Ayodhya, Mathura and Varanasi (Benares, state of Uttar Pradesh), Dwarka (state of Gujarat), Kanchipuram and Ramesvaram (state of Tamil Nadu), derive their holiness from their situation on the banks of a river or near to a stretch of water. They thus have a *tirtha* (literally 'ford'), a sacred place which draws crowds of pilgrims, since by taking a ritual bath in the sacred waters one can become free of the cycle of *samsara*. In India, almost ever river is more or less sacred. Consequently, cities located at the confluence (*sangam*) of several watercourses enjoy an even greater aura of sanctity. This is the case with the city of Prayag, sited at the confluence of the Ganges and the Jamuna, the two most sacred rivers of India, and towards which the mythical and subterranean Sarasvati also flows. This exceptional situation confers on the city the glorious title of *tirtharaja* (literally 'king of the rivers'). To go on pilgrimage to Prayag and to bathe at the confluence of the two rivers brings considerable merits. The Mahabharata already says that the man who bathes in the confluence of the Ganges and the Yamuna will gain the fruits of ten sacrifices of horses, and moreover will save his line. It was at the confluence of these two rivers that on 11 February 1948 the ashes of Mahatma Gandhi, escorted by many boats, were cast on the waters.

4. Historical perspectives

As the ancient Vedic structure disappeared (around the fifth/fourth century BCE), post-Vedic Hinduism progressively gave way to ancient Brahmanism. It covered an extremely long period of almost twenty-five centuries. These can be divided into five main phases, each corresponding to five key moments in the history of India.

The first phase after Vedic times is identified with the 'Hindu synthesis' which, as we saw, extends to the end of the epic period (around the third and fourth centuries CE). It corresponds to the period during which new literary sources became established. These accompanied the renewal of the pantheon (the rise of Shiva and Vishnu) and of cultic practices, while at the beginning of the Christian era the *darshanas* (literally 'points of view [on reality]'), doctrines of the traditional schools of Brahmanic thought based both on the Vedic revelation (*sruti*) and on the texts of tradition (*smrti*), entered a new phase of their history.

This initial phase was followed by the era of classical Hinduism, during which the Puranas were edited; at the same time the texts of tradition based on memory (*smrti*) were codified. Furthermore, at the beginning of the Christian era the *darshanas* were made foundation texts, and from the eighth century they were to become the object of commentaries written by particularly prolific authors. The classical phase extends for almost one thousand years and ends with the establishment of Islam in India (the sultanate of Delhi in 1206).

The third historical phase corresponds to Muslim domination (thirteenth to eighteenth centuries). The era of the sultanate of Delhi (1206–1525) is marked by forced conversions to Islam, which gave converts access to government posts and authorized privileges. Despite conflicts between Muslims and Hindus directly linked to the politics of the particular sultan, contact between the two communities nevertheless allowed exchanges of ideas and interpenetration of religious traditions. With the rise of the Moghul empire, the religious climate became somewhat calmer, particularly during the tolerant reigns of Akbar (1556–1605) and his son Jahangir (1605–1627). In northern India, the sixteenth century is marked by a renaissance of Hinduism and more specifically of Krishnaite *bhakti,* thanks to the preaching of two great mystics,

Chaitanya (1486–1533) in Bengal and in Orissa, and Vallabha (1479–1531) around Mathura, and also mystical poets like the princess Mirabai (1498–1546) in Rajasthan and Gujarat and Sur-Das (c.1530–c.1610) near Mathura. In the Maratha country, mention must be made of the work of Tukaram (1598–1650), the illiterate poet. At the same time the work of the poet Tulsi-Das (died 1623) was to confer especial splendour on the Ramaite tendency. Kabir (died 1518), another illiterate mystical poet, doubly influenced by Islam and Hinduism, whose work was first transmitted orally before being written down, rejected the claims of the religious systems to reveal the divine mystery, castigated the hypocrisy of the religious of his time and preached a revelation of the silent word (*sabda*) pronounced by the perfect guru (*Satguru* = god) in the depth of the soul. The confrontation between Islam and Hinduism also gave birth to the Sikh religion founded by Guru Nanak (1469–1539).

Muslim domination was succeeded by British colonization (1757–1947). This fourth period is marked by different Reform movements in Hinduism (the Hindu revival) inaugurated by Ram Mohan Roy (1772–1833), and by the renaissance of Indian culture under the aegis of figures like the poet and dramatist Rabindranath Tagore (1861–1941). The spiritual influence of Hinduism began to extend abroad, particularly thanks to Swami Vivekananda (1863–1902), who introduced one of the greatest figures of nineteenth-century Hindu mysticism, Sri Ramakrishna (1836–1886), to the West and the United States.

The last phase begins with Independence in 1947. This phase is marked on the one hand by the vitality of worship which, despite the modernization of the country, still remains very present in the everyday life of the Hindu masses, and on the other hand by the appearance in Europe and the United States of a multitude of Hindu gurus who since the 1960s have left their homeland to spread their message abroad. Furthermore, fertile exchanges begun in the early 1940s by Fr Jules Monchanin made it possible to have real inter-religious dialogue between Christians and Hindus, which was carried forward by Henri Le Saux and Bede Griffiths. Finally, mention should be made of the problems posed to Indian democracy since the middle of the 1980s by the renaissance of militant Hinduism in the form of Hindu nationalism directed against the Muslim community in the country. The spectacular destruction of the Babri mosque in Ayodhya in December 1992 is a tragic illustration of this.

This history, the main stages of which are indicated above, is far from being linear, because of the many branches which constitute the Hindu current. Consequently it cannot be presented in a few clear and precise pages, since numerous shadowy areas remain, still hiding some aspects of its development. As for the early period, several questions still remain unanswered. For example, it is not totally clear how the internal transformations came about at the beginning of the Christian era which ended by changing the face of Brahmanism, sometimes profoundly. In the same way, for want of precise documents, it is difficult to understand how the encounter came about between the Hindu current and the indigenous religious traditions with which it was confronted at the time of the Hinduization of the country.

All these questions are complicated by the very structure of Hinduism, which has no central dogmatic authority nor orthodoxy, but is fragmented into a multitude of sects (*sampradaya*, literally 'transmission' = line). While the majority of these have found a place in the Shivaite or Vishnuite traditions, they nevertheless have their own history. It is important to emphasize that these sectarian movements, the history of which cannot be related here, correspond neither to exclusivist or schismatic groups favouring separation from the great tradition of Hinduism, nor even to movements which are hostile to one another. The best indication of this is that they have rarely been in conflict over the course of their long history, despite an extraordinary promiscuity.

The Hindu 'sects', which comprise only a part of the mass of faithful, reflect the traditional condi-

The 'Ayodhya Affair'

Ayodhya is a small town in the Indian state of Uttar Pradesh, in the conurbation of Faizabad, on the river Ghangara, a tributary of the Ganges, about 120 miles north-west of Benares.

In the Ramayana, Ayodhya is the brilliant capital of king Dasaratha, father of Rama. Rama, one of the incarnations of Vishnu, is a key figure in popular and devotional Hinduism, particularly in northern India. He is the model of the good prince, and the utopia of a perfect government is defined as the 'reign of Rama' (*Ram Rajya*). Ayodhya, where Rama was born, is therefore one of the seven holy cities of Hinduism. Among its extremely numerous temples, that built on the supposed birthplace of Rama (*Ram Janmabhumi*) is said to have been destroyed and replaced in 1524 by a mosque bearing the name of the first of the great Moghuls, Baber (*Babri Masjid*), a presumption challenged by a number of historians for want of absolutely conclusive proof.

Along with the militant Hindu movements, the Bharatiya Janata Party (BJP) waged a political campaign, which was intensified in 1990, for a monumental temple to be built on the site of the mosque, and this was prepared for by a number of marches. The mosque was finally destroyed on 6 December 1992 by a mob summoned from all over India, with the complicity of the BJP government of Uttar Prahesh. The central government did not foresee the attack. This destruction, followed by riots which left more than 1,500 people dead throughout the country, made plain to all how radical Hindu nationalism had become, and how great was the ideological crisis of a country which was asking questions about its future. Could India continue to manage its religious pluralism on the basis of the secularity recognized as the foundation of the nation since Independence, or could it, if the BJP came out on top in the long term, redefine itself as a Hindu state with a tendency towards fundamentalism?

The place selected for action was a highly symbolic choice, because of its roots not only in history, but also in myth and epic. The nationalists did not only aim at a heritage of Indian Islam. They chose to act by attacking a holy village which, even more than Benares, another target that was announced, associated with its religious dimension the powerful political charge of the divine figure of Rama, the good prince who was the guarantor of good civil and cosmic order.

(Jean-Luc Racine, 'Ayodhya', in Yves Lacoste [ed.], *Dictionnaire de géopolitique*, 232).

tions of ancient Brahmanism. Consequently, in a Hindu context 'sect' denotes any movement founded by an exemplary personality with recognized sanctity who, within the tradition, chooses to honour one or other deity more specially. This deity thus becomes 'the' deity of the group, while being perceived most often as a manifestation or a form of the major deities Shiva or Vishnu. A group which has chosen one or another part of the tradition does not separate from the Hindu mainstream, nor does it reject its main principles. On the other hand, it can choose a book to which it accords a quite special veneration and practise certain special rites in its specific sanctuaries. Some external signs can also serve to make it known, like the three horizontal bars traced on the foreheads and arms of Shivaite adepts and the marks in the form of a U or Y on the foreheads of Vishnuites.

III
Hinduism in the Modern World

The period of Muslim domination (thirteenth to eighteenth centuries) was much longer than the two centuries of British colonization (1757–1947). However, the impact of Western civilization on Indian culture was deeper than the stamp left by Islam in India, despite the considerable cultural heritage that Islam bequeathed to it. Not only did the West mark the economic and political structures of the country to a greater degree than Islam did in the period of its domination, but above all Hindu religion and modes of thought were challenged on their own ground by the assaults of Western culture. If the English were not the first Westerners to establish themselves in India, it was principally through them that Western civilization gained a foothold on the sub-continent, in particular after their definitive settlement in Bengal in 1765. It is thought that the contacts established during previous centuries by other Western countries remained limited, since they only affected coastal zones (trading posts), and outside them Western influence remained minimal. This chapter will describe the reform movements which came to be organized during the nineteenth century in order to offer solutions to the problems posed by the confrontation between Hinduism and Western culture and survey the major spiritual figures of modern and contemporary Hinduism. We shall then look at some of the Hindu gurus and try to understand why they have been so successful in Europe and the United States from the 1960s onwards. Finally, we shall look at the career of Fr H. Le Saux, a pioneer of interfaith dialogue between Hinduism and Christianity.

Around the 1830s, small groups of intellectuals emerged in Bengal. They set out to examine their own tradition and to compare it with Western culture, eliminating outdated elements. They thought it necessary to adapt the Hindu context to a West which could not be assimilated, and to reform society and some outmoded religious practices without losing their souls or their identities. Because of the attitude that they adopted towards the West and what they kept of their own tradition, these groups, which subsequently became movements of social and religious reform, belonged either to the traditionalist current embodied by the Arya Samaj or to the reform and modernist current of Ram Mohan Roy.

1. Reform movements and contemporary 'masters'

The first Indian intellectual to become aware of the need to reform certain Hindu religious practices and to modernize the country was a Bengali Brahmin, Ram Mohan Roy (1772–1833). After a linguistic training at Patna which enabled him to master English, Arabic and Persian, he became interested in religions, in particular Islam, Christianity and Buddhism, which he studied in their respective languages. Then he taught at Benares before working for the British administration of his country from 1803 to 1813. After this, he withdrew to Calcutta, living on his fortune and devoting all his time and energy to social and religious reforms.

In 1814 he created the Atmya Sabha ('Society of Friends'), which met regularly for spiritual reading and debates. In 1828, he founded the Brahmasabha, later called Brahma Samaj ('Society of the Supreme Being'), the aim of which was to stir up within Hinduism a reform which would allow it to rediscover its original form.

Roy's religious doctrine in fact sought to return to the sources of Hinduism. He interpreted the Vedic texts in a theistic sense and wanted to restore the tradition of the Upanishads organized around the figure of Brahman, whose supremacy as supreme and eternal being he sought to establish. He fought vigorously against the cult of images, claiming that it was the purest superstition and contrary both to reason and to common sense. He also rejected 'Hindu polytheism', and never ceased to affirm his belief in a single God, inaccessible and eternal, who could only be addressed in worship. Despite some sympathy for Christianity, which in his view embodied an ethical code, he remained fundamentally persuaded that it was the Upanishads that best expressed the eternal truths. He gave a key place to the figure of Christ, because for him Christ was the ideal moral teacher. However, he rejected the divinity of Christ, since only God can be God. Jesus is no more God than the avatars which manifest the descent of the divine. Moreover, for Roy, to affirm the Trinity was to risk lapsing into the error of polytheism.

Socially, Ram Mohan Roy took up the question of the condition of Indian women by contributing actively to the suppression of the custom of suttee (the sacrifice of widows on the funeral pyres of their husbands). This was abolished in Bengal in 1829. He also argued for the remarriage of widows and fought against the social abuses of polygamy. In the sphere of education he was an ardent promoter of scientific teaching, contributing towards the inclusion of subjects like mathematics, chemistry and the natural sciences in school curricula. He also played an active part in promoting the vernacular, emphasizing that children had to be educated in their mother tongue. To this end he edited a grammar of Bengali to promote his regional language. He was also the first journalist, the founder of newspapers and periodicals in English and in Persian, and a passionate defender of the freedom of the press. His work includes several books in which he expresses his reforming and modernist zeal, and translations into Bengali or English of the Vedanta Sutra, the main Upanishads and even extracts from the Gospels (*The Precepts of Jesus*).

After his death in England in 1833, the Brahma Samaj survived, thanks to Roy's friends, notably Dvarkanath Tagore (died 1846). His son, Devendranath Tagore (1817–1905), who in 1839 had founded a society with marked Hindu monotheistic tendencies, joined the Samaj in 1842. In 1843 he endowed it with statutes and a book, the *Brahmadharma*, which brought together extracts from the Upanishads and various Hindu texts. After 1850 he gave up the idea of the infallibility of the Veda, and it seems that from this date his society returned to more orthodox practices.

In 1857, the arrival in the Brahma Samaj of Keshab Chandra Sen (1838–1884) brought about a renewal of the movement, but also led to dissent which ended up in a number of schisms. In fact Sen, who rapidly made a mark with his enthusiasm and his eloquence, suggested a radical modification of the general lines of the movement. In 1865 he fell out with the old members of the society, particularly Debendranath Tagore, who then founded the Adibrahma Samaj. Sen rejected the distinction between the castes, affirmed his faith in one God, and found room for rites inspired by Christianity (baptism and Bible readings). Parting company with the old members, he founded the Brahma Samaj of India.

Sen made himself the most zealous propagandist of the society, arranging series of conferences in Bombay, Pune and Madras, and sending missionaries throughout the country. This gave the Brahma Samaj a national audience. The radical positions which he supported (the abolition of child marriages, the education of women, legalization of marriage between the castes) put him in the first rank of the social reformers. So it was that in 1872 he contributed to the publication of the Native Marriage Act, which recognized civil marriage and authorized the remarriage of widows.

From 1875, the time when he first met Ramakrishna, he abandoned social action to preach a new divine law, The New Dispensation. However, in 1878 another schism developed because of the marriage of his younger daughter to the son of a Maharajah, and his detractors then founded the Sadharanbrahma Samaj (literally 'common Brahma Samaj'). In 1881, Sen's tendency adopted the name Navavidhan (New Dispensation Church). This new religion, which its founder put on an equal footing with Jewish, Christian and Vishnuite revelations, was a syncretism of elements borrowed from Islam, Christianity, Vishnuism (devotional mysticism inspired by Chaitanya) and Shivaism (the cult of Durga).

Sen's devotion to the person of Jesus – he presented himself as Jesudas (literally 'servant of Jesus') – recalls the emotional accents of *bhakti*. His theology (the conception of an Asian Christ), above all his christology (the doctrine of a divine humanity) and his trinitarian doctrine, remained very personal and often ambiguous, which led to it being compared with certain Christian heresies (like Arianism) which had been condemned by the first ecumenical councils. After his death in 1884, his church rapidly lost influence because of internal dissent.

From the 1870s onwards, the various branches of the Samaj lost their attraction. They were challenged by traditionalist movements which thought that Hinduism could rediscover its original identity and reform itself from within without confronting either the West or Christianity. From this date we also find the first signs of a cultural nationalism, and the Brahma Samaj became above all philanthropic societies devoted to social (education) or charitable works.

The movement which best embodied this traditionalist religion was organized around Mul Sankar (1824–1833), in religion Dayananda Sarasvati, a Brahmin from Gujarat. Brought up in an orthodox Shivaite milieu, at a very early age he showed an independent mind and soon rebelled against both the authority of his father and the daily religious rites which he had to perform scrupulously. The starting point of his revolt is frequently identified as the experience he had during his youth in the vigils of the night of Shiva (Shiva Ratri) during which he saw in a temple a mouse eating the offerings set before the statue and then running over the body of the idol. As a result of this incident, he came to believe that in venerating images Hinduism had departed from the authentic Vedic tradition which alludes neither to temples nor to images.

In order to escape an arranged marriage, he decided to leave his family home. Between 1845 and 1860–1863 he travelled all over India in search of a guru, devoting himself to yogic practices and visiting places of pilgrimage. During this journey he became aware of the problems of his country (poverty, illiteracy, superstitions) and the changes that British colonialism had imposed on Indian civilization. At Mathura he finally met the man who was to inspire him with his definitive vocation, the blind ascetic Swami Virjananda Sarasvati. He stayed with this learned and demanding master for three years, and before bidding him farewell promised that he would devote his life to disseminating the authentic principles of Hinduism by bringing about a return to the Veda.

In his addresses and his sermons, Dayananda Sarasvati also showed interest in reforms. For example, he denounced child marriage, and argued for marriage with free consent (*svayamvara* marriage), which he considered 'the earliest form of marriage in India, and also the best' (*Satyarthaprakasa*, ch. IV), and for the education of children, especially daughters. However, his standpoints were above all a pretext for claiming that the religious and social inadequacies of the Hinduism of his day castigated by Western criticism did not exist in the Vedic period. To focus his projects and give shape to his doctrine he founded the Arya Samaj ('Society of the Arya') in Bombay in 1875. The first three points of the decalogue on which the society was based contain the theological basis of his system:

– God [the Supreme Lord = *paramesvara*] is the first cause of all true knowledge and of what this knowledge reveals to us.
– God is perfect truth, knowledge and bliss: incorporeal, omnipotent, just, merciful, uncreated, infinite, immutable, without beginning, incomparable, the support and lord of all, penetrating all, omniscient, imperishable, immortal, without fear, eternal and holy. He is the cause of the universe and he alone is worthy of being adored.
– The Vedas are the books of the true knowledge and it is the first duty of every *arya* to read them or listen to them, to teach them and read them to others.

The other seven points define an individual and social morality which each member of the Arya Samaj must make his own. 4. Every *arya* must always be ready to accept the truth and reject the lie. 5. Everything must be done in conformity with *dharma*. 6. The principal aim of the Arya Samaj is to be useful to the whole world, in other words to contribute to the physical, spiritual and social condition of humankind. 7. All must be treated with love and justice, taking account of their merits. 8. It is important to dissipate ignorance and spread knowledge. 9. No one should confine himself to seeking his own happiness; each should consider that his own well-being is intimately bound up with that of others. 10. No one should allow himself to harm the general good, but in strictly personal matters each can act freely.

It is by reading the *Satyarthaprakasa* ('The Light of Truth'), his most famous work, that we can see what distinguishes the positions of Dayananda Sarasvati from those of the Brahma Samaj. For the founder of the Arya Samaj, the four Vedas (Rig Veda, Yajur Veda, Sama Veda, Atharva Veda) are infallible, and their superiority over all other Hindu texts is unchallengable. By contrast, he considered the commentaries on the four Vedas (the Brahmanas) secondary works with authority only to the degree that they were in conformity with the Vedas. He presented Vedic religion as a rigorous monotheism allowing no place for polytheism or the Hindu cult of images, because the supreme deity was perceived as Absolute. In his view the thirty-three deities (*devatas*) mentioned in the Veda, though called *devatas*, are only the forces of nature or activities with some useful qualities. They never represent *the* deity, the supreme Being, whom he called the thirty-fourth *devata* and who alone was to be the object of adoration.

As described by Dayananda Sarasvati, Vedic times tended to be transformed into a glorious golden age in which the Arya appeared as an elect people opposed to the *dasyus* (who were wicked, heretical and brutal). They were said to have come down from the regions of Tibet after creation because of the wars between the Arya and the *dasyus*. They migrated into the Aryavarta ('the abode of the Arya'), 'considering this country the best on earth', virgin land uninhabited before their arrival, bounded on the north by the chain of the Himalayas, on the south by the Vindhya range, on the West by the Indus and on the east by the Brahmaputra.

Sarasvati was opposed to the other religions, notably Islam and Christianity, accusing them of conveying false truths and of wanting to destroy Hinduism. He also wanted to purify Hinduism from elements alien to its Vedic source which had been added by history, and to purge it of iconolatry.

After the death of its founder in 1883 the movement continued to expand. The Arya Samaj had only 40,000 members in 1891, but claimed more than 1 million by 1931. It proved most successful in the Punjab, where it made a lasting mark. By contrast, it had little influence in southern India and, like the Brahma Samaj of Ram Mohan Roy, the Arya Samaj touched only a fraction of the population, the educated urban classes. The movement helped to create schools and colleges (like the Dayananda Anglo-Vedic College of Lahore) and humanitarian institutions (hospitals).

The spiritual current deriving from Ramakrishna (1836–1886) formed a very different way from the reforming and modernist Brahma Samaj and the more traditionalist Arya Samaj. Entirely centred on religious experience, the life of Ramakrishna is that of a Hindu saint, perhaps the greatest saint of the nineteenth century, who takes his place in the long tradition of *bhakti*.

Contrary to the two precedents mentioned above, Ramakrishna was not concerned to reform society. He even emphasized the importance of leaving things as they are, believing that the only important thing is to realize God.

Through his holiness, which was recognized during his lifetime, he contributed to restoring confidence in their own tradition to the Indians. For many of them he is the embodiment of the vitality of Hinduism at the heart of the modern world, allied with a breadth of vision and an extreme religious tolerance, a profound faith with a moving sincerity.

Gadadhar Chattopadhyaya was born in 1836 of a poor family of pious Brahmans who came from Bengal, in the village of Kamarpukur in the Hugli district. Around the age of six he experienced his first mystical ecstasy and at the age of nine he was initiated as a Brahmin. Around the age of sixteen he unsuccessfully helped his older brother Ramkumar, who had just opened a Sanskrit school in Calcutta and also served as priest for rich families in the capital of Bengal. At the same time a rich and pious widow who had just had a temple dedicated to the goddess Kali built near Calcutta at Dakshineswar was having great difficulties, because of her lowly status, in finding a Brahmin priest to serve in the temple. After some hesitation, Ramkumar accepted the ministry, but died a year later. In 1856, despite only a rudimentary school education and theological training, Ramakrishna succeeded his brother and at the age of twenty served at this temple.

Shortly after his installation, Ramakrishna often fell into ecstasy, and Kali, the divine mother, appeared to him so often that he even forgot his duties as a priest. He maintained a continual mystical intimacy with the goddess and practised a deliriously devotional cult to her. He neither slept nor ate normally, to the point that his health was seriously affected. The visitors to the temple did not understand the strange behaviour of this mystical priest who was 'crazy about God' and he was thought to be mad. Medical treatment was even prescribed for him, and in May 1859 his family arranged a marriage for him with Sarada Devi (1853–1920), a very young girl of five, in order to distract his spirit from the mystical world. Eighteen months later, when his health had improved, he returned to Dakshineswar, where the mystical delirium took over again.

For almost ten years, this time under the spiritual direction of several gurus, he began to undertake a systematic exploration of the different spiritual courses of Hinduism. An ascetic Brahmin versed in Tantric techniques first initiated him into Tantric yoga and reassured him of the quality of his previous experiences. She taught him that he had gone through the highest stages of mystic life and had even attained *mahabhava*, the supreme and ecstatic love of God.

A wandering monk called Tota Puri, an adept of Advaita Vedanta (non-dualistic Vedanta), taught him to transcend the personal God (Brahman without attributes) in order to attain the Absolute,

> # The Teaching of Ramakrishna
>
> 'The more you come to love God, the less you will be inclined to perform action. When a daughter-in-law is with child, her mother-in-law gives her less work to do. As time goes by she is given less and less work. When the time of delivery nears, she is not allowed to do any work at all, lest it should hurt the child or cause difficulty at the time of birth.
>
> By these philanthropic activities you are really doing good to yourself. If you can do them disinterestedly, your mind will become pure and you will develop love of God. As soon as you have that love, you will realize Him.
>
> Man cannot really help the world. God alone does that – He who has created the sun and the moon, who has put love for their children in parents' hearts, who has endowed noble souls with compassion, and holy men and devotees with divine love. The man who works for others, without any selfish motive, really does good to himself.'
>
> 'It is not good to feel that my religion alone is true and other religions are false. The correct attitude is this: My religion is right, but I do not know whether other religions are right or wrong, true or false. I say this because one cannot know the true nature of God unless one realizes Him . . .
>
> Do you know what the truth is? God has made different religions to suit different aspirants, times, and countries. All doctrines are only so many paths; but a path is by no means God Himself. Indeed, one can reach God if one follows any of the paths with whole-hearted devotion. Suppose there are errors in the religion that one has accepted; if one is sincere and earnest, then God Himself will correct those errors. If there are errors in other religions, that is none of our business. God, to whom the world belongs, takes care of that.'
>
> (*The Gospel of Sri Ramakrishna*, pp.162, 336)

which has neither name nor form (Brahman without attributes). Following this second initiation, in a state of transcendental consciousness, he succeeded in realizing the union of *atman* with the Vedantic *brahman*, and remained for six months in the *nirvikalpa-samadhi* (literally 'changeless *samadhi*'), the highest state of mystic ecstasy (*The Teaching of Ramakrishna*, 1491). He realized in his being the *tat tvam asi* – 'you are that' – of the Chandogya Upanishad.

At the same time he also continued to study the spiritual ways of other religions, which he wanted to experience from within, considering them also to be spiritual disciplines (*sadhanas*). Under the guidance of a Muslim named Govinda Rai, in 1866 he undertook the practice of Muslim disciplines, in particular training himself to repeat the name of Allah, and in a vision came to contemplate the face of the Prophet Muhammad. Some years later, when he was looking at a pious image representing the Virgin and the child Jesus, the image came to life in a vision for him.

At the end of these personal mystical experiences, all of which led to inner illumination, Ramakrishna arrived at the idea of the transcendent unity of the religions. He explained that at a superior mystical level all the religions are different ways leading to one and the same end, the Absolute which reveals itself by an avatar, 'the play of the Infinite in the finite'. Depending on the time and place this is called Rama, Krishna, Jesus. His message is a great appeal for religious tolerance.

As the renown of Ramakrishna's holiness spread in the region of Calcutta, the temple of Dakshineswar attracted a great many visitors, and several of them became his disciples. From 1875 on, Keshab Chandra Sen paid several visits to the saint; he was certainly deeply impressed by the religious universalism of Ramakrishna, as is shown by the eclecticism which he showed when he began to preach his universal religion (New Dispensation Church).

The most famous disciple of Ramakrishna, who was to devote his whole life to making the doctrine of his master known, was beyond question Naredranath Datta (1863–1902), better known under his religious name of Swami Vivekananda. Born into a rich Bengali family in Calcutta, Vivekananda was a young and brilliant intellectual, open to Western ideas. At a very early age he belonged to the Brahma Samaj. In November 1881, at the home of a disciple of Ramakrishna, he met his future guru for the first time. Impressed both by the sincerity of the young man and his desire to know God, Ramakrishna invited him to pay a visit to his temple. Vivekananda soon recognized that he had at last found a true master and became his disciple – very soon the preferred disciple. Five years later, before his death, Ramakrishna entrusted Vivekananda with the continuation of his work. At the end of 1886, Vivekananda laid down the foundations of a monastic order, the Order of Ramakrishna, which he established at Baranagore (between Calcutta and Dakshineswar). It remained there until 1892, and in 1898 was finally settled in the suburb of Belur Math, north of Calcutta.

After the death of his master, Vivekananda travelled through India, criss-crossing the sub-continent from north to south, going up the Ganges, and visiting the Himalayas, the Rajputana and South India. Following a vision which he had at Cape Comorin that seemed to push him towards the New World, he decided to leave for the United States with a view to representing Hinduism and the Veda at the Parliament of the World's Religions in Chicago, though he himself did not represent any religious institution. On 31 May 1893, thanks to the support of his friends and the financial generosity of the Maharajah of Khetri, he embarked at Bombay on the *Peninsular* for a voyage which took him first to Colombo, then to Hong Kong, to Canton and to Japan before he finally reached Vancouver, from where he travelled to Chicago by train.

Vivekananda received a triumphant welcome at the Parliament of Religions, since as an eloquent and noble orator, he could find the right words to captivate and move his audience. Before this unprecedented success he undertook a series of lectures on Indian philosophy and yoga in the United

33. Ramakrishna (1836–1886)

States, and then had a first stay in Europe, in England. On his return to America in 1896 he founded the Vedanta Society of New York, which was to make known to the United States the Neo-Vedantic teaching of Ramakrishna and Indian philosophy. A second stay in Europe allowed him to visit Switzerland and Germany and to meet the great Orientalists of the time (M. Müller and P. Deussen). After a stay of almost four years in the West, he returned to India, where he received a hero's welcome. In the meantime he had rallied Westerners to his cause, and some of these did not hesitate to follow him to India. His most famous disciple, Margaret Noble (1867–1911), who took the habit of a renunciant under the name of Sister Nivedita ('she who has been dedicated'), devoted herself to the education of young girls and the teaching of Indian women.

34. Swami Vivekananda (1863–1902)

On his return to Bengal in 1897, Swami Vivekananda founded the Ramakrishna Mission in Calcutta, a religious organization called to be the spearhead in spreading the thought of Ramakrishna both in India and abroad. It established several monasteries (*maths*) in India, but also in the United States and in Europe.

Like Ramakrishna, Swami Vivekananda was deeply convinced that all the religions are true and that if there are differences between them, they relate to non-essential points. However, while affirming the superiority of India and the East over the materialist West and preaching in certain texts that the ideal of the Hindus must be the spiritual conquest of the whole world for its edification, he was sometimes led to envisage a militant Hinduism of which there is no trace in Ramakrishna. Furthermore, he emphasized that disinterested action (in particular social action) leads to individual liberation, an ideal which he tended to substitute for that of devotion (*bhakti*), which was the heart of his master's thought.

During the twentieth century, India has produced some distinguished religious figures: intellectuals (Rabindrath Tagore, died 1941); political and social reformers (M. K. Gandhi, died 1948; V. Bhave, died 1982); philosophers (S. Dasgupta, died 1952; S. Radhakrishnan, died 1975; and T. Mahadevan, born 1911); and also great ascetics and authentic mystics, great men of God who have perpetuated the immemorial tradition of the guru down to the modern age. Most of these masters were born during the last three decades of the nineteenth century and were recognized during their lifetime; from their ashrams groups of disciples spread their message, some of them Westerners.

Since we cannot look in detail at the lives and teachings of all these gurus in the present book, I have chosen to concentrate on two striking figures as a first introduction.

Ramana Maharshi (1879–1950) has unanimously been recognized as one of the greatest representatives of contemporary Hindu spirituality, and his reputation rapidly spread beyond the frontiers of India. Born in a Brahmin family in a village in South India near Madurai, where his father was the village lawyer, Venkataraman Aiyar, later to be known as Maharshi (literally 'great sage') – Ramana is a contraction of his first name Venkata *raman* – was not a very brilliant pupil and was little versed in the study of the sacred texts. At the age of seventeen, he had an inner experience which turned his life upside down. Without any books and without the help of any master, he had an experience of Being. Alone in his uncle's house, he suddenly found himself invaded by fear of his own death which turned his thoughts inwards. What is death? What does it mean to die? During his internal crisis, the young Venkataraman came to understand that

Gandhi

Mahatma Gandhi (1869–1941) is certainly the best-known Hindu in the West, though for a long time he was misunderstood.

The key to his personality and his action is given to us by a very simple formula which he himself produced: 'Man is under the obligation to be guided by moral considerations in all his actions.' And if one goes on to ask what he understood by moral considerations, it is enough to report the kind of creed which he pronounced at home before every meal: 'Non-violence, truth, refraining from stealing, chastity, having no possessions, physical work, inactivity of the taste organs, lack of fear, equal respect for all religions, *svadesi*, a spirit of brotherhood without exclusiveness – these eleven desires must be observed in a spirit of humility'.

The starting point of his morality was naturally provided by his religion, which always remained strictly Hindu. As he used to say, 'I am a reformer from the soles of my feet to the crown of my head, but my zeal never drives me to reject any of the essential elements of Hinduism.' And while he fought indefatigably to improve the lot of the 'untouchables', he nevertheless always defended the basic principle of the caste system, which he saw as a 'scientific rational fact' and a 'healthy division of work on the basis of birth'.

His chosen deity was Rama, on whom he constantly modelled himself, and he hardly let a day go by without reading passages from the Ramayana for an hour or more. But in the prayer meetings which he held wherever he went, and to which people flocked by the thousands, often having travelled for dozens of miles on foot, there were recitations of passages not only from the sacred Hindu texts but also from the Bible and the Qur'an.

Whatever his religious preoccupations, however, Gandhi always refused to allow himself to be considered as a religious master – which is difficult in India for a leader followed by crowds.

Non-violence was the principle of Gandhi's which most caught the imagination of the world. He made it an intransigent conception going far beyond what the West could understand by it. 'The principle of *ahimsa*,' he wrote, 'is infringed by any evil thought, any unjustified haste, by lies, hatred, ill-will towards anyone. It is equally violated when one keeps for oneself something that the world needs.' But non-violence does not mean laxity; quite the contrary, as he himself proved when submitting, with his numerous disciples, to blows from the police and imprisonment. '*Ahimsa* is not the way of the timid or the cowardly. It is the way of the brave ready to face death. He who perishes sword in hand is no doubt brave, but he who faces death without raising his little finger is braver. But he who surrenders his rice bags for fear of being beaten is a coward and no votary of *ahimsa*. He is innocent of *ahimsa*. He who, for fear of being beaten, suffers the women of his household to be insulted, is not manly but quite the reverse. He is fit to be be neither a husband nor a father nor a brother.'

It is only in the light of these principles, which are all classic principles of Hinduism, that one can understand the actions of Gandhi in the public, social and economic spheres. He only engaged in these activities by defending them with his body, and was always guided by those 'moral considerations' which were an imperative for him. He thought the material consequences which might ensue from them for himself or others to be a secondary matter.

In politics, his great directive was the famous prayer, 'Lord, lead India along the way of truth.' In his economic action, which was more important than his political action, but which is less known and much less understood in the West, he was of course guided by the same preoccupations. His opposition to industrialization of a Western kind was the logical consequence of his desire to see his compatriots lead the individualist, rural and patriarchal life which suited them instead of subjecting themselves to the frightful impoverishment of the industrial centres and the immorality which inevitably developed there.

(Jean Hebert, *L'Hindouisme vivant*, 257–9)

> # Ramana Maharshi on Death and Immortality
>
> This body is dead. It will be carried, quite stiff, to the place of cremation, where it will be burned and reduced to ashes. But with the death of this body, am *I* dead? Is the body *me*? This body is silent and inert. But I feel the whole force of my personality and even 'self' within me, apart from the body. So I am a spirit, something which transcends the body.
>
> I am an immortal spirit. All this was not a simple intellectual process. All this flashed before me as the living truth, something that I perceived immediately, almost irrationally. I was something very real, the only real thing in this state, and all my conscious activity in relation to my body was centred on this thing. From that moment the I or Self became the focus of attention of an all-powerful fascination. The fear of death vanished once and for all. Absorption in the Self continued from then on. Other thoughts can come and go, like the different notes played by a musician, but the Self goes on as a bass which accompanies all the others and is fused with them.

when the material body dies, the transcendent spirit cannot be affected by death.

This experience marked the second part of his life. Soon afterwards he left his family home and, feeling himself called by the holy mountain of Arunachala which dominates the city of Tiruvannamalai (Tamil Nadu), he withdrew there until the end of his life. He settled first in the temple of Arunachala, then in several caves on the side of the mountain, and finally, after the death of his mother in 1922, below the mountain, near his tomb around which the *ashram* developed. R. Maharshi wrote little and never sought to spread any kind of structured or systematic teaching. When visitors came to see him, he simply asked the question 'Who are you?', to stimulate them to seek the self within them.

35. Ramana Maharshi (1879–1950)

The career of Aurobindo Ghose, called by his disciples Sri Aurobindo (1872–1950), was very different from that of the sage of Arunachala. He was born in Calcutta in a well-to-do family. His father, a doctor and fervent admirer of Europe and England, wanted his children to receive the best possible education. So he sent the young Aurobindo at the age of only five to an English school in Darjeeling. Two years later, the Ghose family set sail for England, where Aurobindo pursued his studies in the company of his two brothers. He only returned to India in 1893, and on his return found himself in a foreign country, since he did not know Bengali, the language of his native land.

From 1893 to 1906 he worked in the state administration of Baroda, Gujarat, first in the immigration service, then in the post office, and finally in the tax office. He subsequently became secretary to the Maharajah, then at the same time a teacher of English, and Vice Principal, later Interim Principal, of Baroda College. During these years he devoted his spare time to constructing an Indian and Hindu culture, studying Sanskrit and learning Gujarati and Bengali. In 1906 he resigned his official functions to return to Bengal, where he engaged in feverish political activity. Joining the extremist trend of the Svaraj (a movement for autonomy and independence), he exhorted his compatriots to struggle for the liberation of their country. His inflammatory speeches and violent articles called for nationalist resistance and supported a boycott on English goods in favour of products made in India (*svadesi*). Arrested by the British authorities at the beginning of May 1908 on a charge of being involved in a terrorist plot against the district judge at Muzaffarpur which the previous month had cost the lives of two English, he spent a year in Alipore prison. During his imprisonment he devoted himself to meditation and to the study of the Bhagavad Gita and the Upanishads. At his trial in May 1909 he was found not guilty and released. After much soul-searching, he decided to withdraw from the political struggle. Free, but again threatened with arrest, he forestalled the plans of the British government and took refuge in French territory at Pondicherry (4 April 1910). There he remained until his death. He spent the years 1910 to 1914 in meditation and yoga, going out very little and receiving hardly any visitors. In August 1914, thanks to the support of the Frenchman Paul Richard, he founded the philosophical monthly *Arya*, which until 1921 published his most important works in article form.

In 1921 some disciples gathered round him, and from 1926, an ashram took shape. Under the influence of Richard's Turco-Egyptian wife, Mirra Alfassa (1878–1973), whom his disciples called 'the Mother', the Sri Aurobindo Ashram steadily grew. In 1953 it comprised almost 800 disciples, including around a dozen Westerners. From 1926, Sri Aurobindo went into almost total retreat; he appeared only four times a year in public for a ritual *darshan* (literally 'vision' – a meeting or interview between the master and his disciples).

After the Master's death in 1950, the Mother ensured that his work would go on. She took over the running of the ashram and in 1951 created the international Sri Aurobindo University centre. From 1954 on she planned the construction of an ideal city, Auroville, in which men and women from all countries could live in peace and harmony regardless of belief, politics or nationality. This project, which received the support of UNESCO, finally began to take shape a few miles from Pondicherry, where the foundation stone was laid in 1968. Young people from more than fifty nations and Indian state put handfuls of earth from their respective counties into an urn. More than twenty-five years after its foundation, this project still has a long way to go, but the roughly 800 inhabitants of Auroville hope to have built the Matri Mandir ('Temple of the Mother'), the centre of the planned city, by the turn of the century.

Aurobindo wrote almost all his books in English; just a few articles, letters and poems were written in Bengali. The key idea of his work is that human beings are the result of the terrestrial evolution of nature from minerals to mind. The process of evolution follows a twofold movement, both outward and inward. The appearance of mind and the human body marks a radical change in the evolutionary process, since it leads to consciousness.

However, and this is the key element in Aurobindo's message, the mind has to be transcended in a rising movement of spiritual transformation. Such a change of awareness is the major feature of the next transformation in the evolutionary chain. With man, however, in contrast to the previous stages of evolution during which the change primarily related to a change of organization which alone can produce a change of consciousness, evolution can and must primarily take place through consciousness, and not through a new bodily organism.

The Teaching of Sri Aurobindo

Mind is not sufficient to explain existence in the universe. Universal consciousness must first translate itself into infinite faculty of knowledge or, as we call it from our point of view, omniscience; but mind is not a faculty of knowledge nor an instrument of omniscience; it is a faculty for the seeking of knowledge, for expressing as much as it can gain of it in certain forms of a relative thought and for using it towards certain capacities of action. Even when it finds, it does not possess; it only keeps a certain fund of current coin of truth – not truth itself – in the bank of memory to draw upon according to its needs. For mind is that which does not know, which tries to know and which never knows except as in a glass darkly. It is the power which interprets truth of universal existence for the practical uses of a certain order of things; it is not the power which knows and guides that existence and therefore it cannot be the power which created or manifested it . . .

But since this consciousness is creatrix of the world, it must be not only state of knowledge, but power of knowledge, and not only a will to light and vision, but a will to power and works. And since mind too is created out of it, mind must be a development by limitation out of this primal faculty and this mediatory act of the supreme consciousness and must therefore be capable of resolving itself back into it through a reverse development by expansion. For always mind must be identical with supermind, . . . however different or even contrary it may have become in its actual forms and settled modes of operation.

(Sri Aurobindo, *The Life Divine*, 109–10, 114–15)

Aurobindo criticizes the form of religion which can easily become a retarding factor when it identifies itself with a creed, a cult, a church or a system of ceremonial forms. By contrast, the true religion seeks to live by the spirit. According to Aurobindo, nature has prepared for the birth of the spiritual man and openness of the inner being by following four main directions: religion, occultism, spiritual thought and inner experience. The first three are approaches, while the fourth is the route by which the decisive entry is made. To achieve this entry, a threefold change is necessary: 1. the soul must take control of the being in its totality; 2. a spiritual transformation must open the being to an Infinite by raising awareness to the overmind, the world of gods and divine beings; 3. when the ascent of the lower consciousness to the superior consciousness can be achieved at will, the new consciousness begins to form and can become permanent and perfect.

Perhaps more than any other figures, Ramana Maharshi and Sri Aurobindo are symbolic figures for contemporary gurus. In different ways they incarnate authentic spiritual values in line with the Vedanta, Maharshi in its strictly non-dualistic form and Aurobindo using a modernized terminology. R. Maharshi recommends to his hearers that they should seek the divine self within them so that they can discover their true identity behind the veils of the individual self. By contrast, Sri Aurobindo does not see individual deliverance as the ultimate aim. He wants to hasten on earth the coming of the gnostic being with the overmind, capable of harmonizing the individual self with the total or cosmic self, a kind of superman who will be 'universal but free in the universe; individual without being limited by a separative individuality' (*The Divine Life*, LV).

After these two figures, at least the names of some contemporary gurus and mystics should be mentioned: Ma Ananda Mayi (1896–1982), an authentic woman mystic whose life was a long and total abandonment to the divine; the Ramaite *bhakta* Swami Ramadasa or Ramdas (1884–1963), whose work was perpetuated by the 'Mother' of his ashram, Krsnabai (1903–1989); Swami Sivananda

2. The advent of gurus in the West

As I have already emphasized, the preaching of Swami Vivekananda on the platform of the Parliament of the World's Religions in 1893 was the starting point for the mission of the Hindu gurus to the West. Fired by his success in Chicago, Vivekananda initiated an educated Western elite into Hindu doctrine and Indian philosophy. He did this first by lectures and courses, and then by setting up the first societies for the study of Vedantic thought (one was founded in New York in 1896). These spread a neo-Vedantic teaching and developed into centres affiliated to the Ramakrishna Mission which Vivekananda founded on his return to India and which were to extend beyond the sub-continent during the first half of the twentieth century. At the same time, through the Theosophical Society and its dissident branches, the key concepts of Hindu thought (*atman, brahman, karma, moksha, samsara*) were disseminated and then polarized in the West, especially in the Anglo-Saxon world, though often in a bastard form, indeed as caricatures.

However, despite the interest which various European or American intellectuals including Romain Rolland, Hermann Hesse and the authors of the Beat Generation showed in the East in general or Hindu thought in particular, the penetration of Hindu ideas and the influence of Eastern religions (Hinduism, Buddhism, Taoism) on Western society remained very limited until the 1960s. From this key date, and simultaneously with the great waves of student revolt, the hippie culture and psychedelic experience, first in the United States and then in Europe various gurus appeared, exalting some aspect or other of Hindu religion in their doctrine. Well received in the anti-intellectualist counter-culture, Hindu concepts and practices became a legitimation of marginalization, or rather elements in a quest for another life-style. The swami teachers of the second phase became the gurus who attracted and then reflected the projections of a frustrated generation.

However, the inadequacies of the Western model

36. Ma Ananda Mayi (1896–1982)

Sarasvati (1887–1963), founder of the Divine Life Society (1936); Swami Prajnanpad (1891–1975), and Sri Nisargadatta Maharaj (1897–1981).

Among living gurus mention should be made of Sri H. W. L. Poonja (born in 1910), a disciple of Maharshi, whose ashram is at Lucknow (Uttar Pradesh). But the most famous of all is without doubt the charismatic but very controversial Sathyanarayan Raju (born 1926), alias Sathya Sai Baba, guru avatar and miracle worker (the materialization of objects and sacred ash [*vibhuti*], healings). His ashram Prasanthi Nilayam (literally 'Abode of Supreme Peace') is at Puttaparthi in Andhra Pradesh, and attracts considerable crowds.

cannot be cited as the only explanation for the phenomenon of the movement of Hindu gurus westwards. Within the framework of the non-academic encounters and exchanges between Hinduism and the West it is quite certain that from the nineteenth-century Theosophists, who sought the foundations of primordial wisdom in an Eastern 'otherness', to the youth revolt of the 1960s, a functional redistribution has taken place between a materialist and technological West on the one hand and a spiritual and traditional East on the other, which has issued in many 'new age' phenomena. However, other facts must be taken into account, since the advent of the guru, first in the new world and then in the old, is no chance phenomenon. In part it is a feature of the Indian response to nineteenth-century colonialism and to the sense of superiority in European culture; it is also the Hindu counterpart to the proselytism of Christian churches in India during the same period. As a result, this contemporary expansion of Hinduism outside the sub-continent is more a feature of the natural cultural interaction between India and the West than a deliberate strategy of conquest, contrary to the fears of some Westerners, who have forgotten rather too quickly the zeal with which the missionaries set out to evangelize the 'pagans' and resent this implantation as a Hindu invasion.

It is worth noting that the cultural encounter and exchange of ideas between the religions has been shaped by a growing Hindu missionary concern. The two cradles of the Hindu mission (the Indus in the north-west and above all Bengal) are the areas where there have been cultural exchanges between the monotheistic religions (Islam and Christianity) and Hinduism. Moreover, most of the gurus attended schools or colleges run by European religious institutions.

Steeped to various degrees in the Reformist ideals of the Hindu revival, the majority of gurus who have settled in the West have taken up the classical themes of neo-Vedantism in their discourses: the oneness of the human soul and the divine, the transcendent unity of the religions and religious universalism, the spiritual superiority of India as the civilization of the sacred and the cradle of religions. If the gurus proclaim the validity and unity of all the religions, it must immediately be added that they always do so from a Hindu perspective begun by Vivekananda, namely by integrating them 'inclusively' into their system in order to neutralize them, without giving them the supreme place in the hierarchy, which always falls to Hinduism.

Of all the new religious movements with a Hindu stamp imported into the West during the 1960s, ISKCON (the International Society for Krishna Consciousness) is certainly the one that the public knows best, under its current name of the 'Hare Krishna Movement'. Everyone has seen its devotees at least once, either in the streets of big cities or on campuses, in Indian dress and playing music on traditional Indian instruments, offering small Indian cakes to passers-by and selling translations of the Bhagavad Gita or collections of teachings from their master.

The Hare Krishna movement, which now has some dozens of centres spread over the five continents, was founded in New York in 1966 by the Bengali Abhay Charan De (1896–1977). It can claim to have roots in a religious heritage going back more than four centuries, since the type of devotion which it seeks to propagate goes back to the Bengali *bhakta* Visvambhara Misra, better known under his religious name of Sri Krishna Chaitanya (1486–1533), to whom the founder of the Hare Krishna movement is directly related.

At some remove from traditional Vishnuism, which makes Krishna one of the many avatars of Vishnu, Chaitanya reversed the perspective and suggested a way of deliverance rich in emotional and affective content, centred on the person of Krishna, who is considered supreme God, master of the universe, existing in himself, and the ultimate expression of the Absolute. Vishnu is relegated to a secondary status. Chaitanya gave his disciples as a model the couple Krishna-Radha, whose union symbolizes above all the union that the faithful has to realize with God (Krishna). To attain the highest state of this participative *bhakti*, establishing a link between man and Krishna which is to lead the devotee to the final deliverance, Chaitanya commended above all the constant practice of the glorification of the holy names of God (= Krishna), individual or corporate, sung and danced, along with the recitation of the famous *maha-mantra* 'Hare Krishna'. Along with this, a disciplined diet and sexual life, and the consuming of food (*prasada*) offered to Lord Krishna can also allow the believer to rise by successive levels to the joy of mystic ecstasy which embraces the whole being and leads the soul to union with the divine.

Before devoting his life entirely to the propagation of Krishna Consciousness, Abhay Charan De in his youth had been close to Gandhi's independence movement. It was out of a policy of non-co-operation with the British that he refused his university diploma before occupying an important position in the Bose pharmaceutical laboratories in Calcutta. In 1932 he was initiated into the forms by Bhaktisiddhanta Sarasvati Thakura (1983–1936) of the spiritual line of Chaitanya. Thakura was the son of Swami Bhaktivinoda Thakura who, at the end of the last century, sought to disseminate the teaching of Chaitanya in India and abroad, explaining that loving devotion to Krishna was the highest form of theism and was the concern of all men, regardless of their case or geographical origin. Shortly before his death in 1935, Swami Baktisiddhanta Sarasvati charged his disciple to reveal to the Western world the religious treasure of Chaitanya's tradition and the philosophy of the Bhagavad Gita.

During the Second World War, in 1944, Abhay Charan De undertook the publication of an English language periodical *Back to Godhead*, which sought to analyse the spiritual crisis of the modern world in the light of texts from the Krishnaite tradition. Having broken with his work and family, in 1959 he acceded to the dignity of *samnyasin* under the name Abhay Caranaravinda Bhaktivedanta Swami. He withdrew to Vrindaban, the high place of Krishnaism, to undertake an English translation of the Bhagavata Purana. At the same time he took up the publication of his journal, becoming its editor, proof-corrector and even its personal distributor. Thanks to the generosity of an Indian businessman, in 1965 he left Calcutta for the New World, where he was to found a movement which became world-wide.

In the United States his disciples suggested that he should add the honorific title Prabhupada (approximately = '[the one who always has] feet in the lotus position [of Krishna] or [the one] at whose feet the prabhu ["masters" prostrate themselves]'), a term which the disciples of a master use among themselves. That is why he is generally called Srila Prabhudapada in the publications of the movement. He died in Vrindaban in the temple of Krishna Balaram on 14 November 1977.

Unlike the founder of the Hare Krishna movment, the founder of Transcendental Meditation, His Holiness Maharishi Mahesh Yogi, has always denied propagating a particular religion or religious ideology. Before we look at the theoretical content and practical forms of the doctrine, let us look briefly at the man and the history of the movement.

Mahesh Prasad Varma was born in India in 1917. After obtaining a licentiate in physics at the University of Allahabad, he gave up scientific studies and turned to a spiritual quest, retiring for twelve years, which 'passed in a flash', with a Vedantic master Swami Brahmananda Sarasvati (1868–1953). Sarasvati taught him a technique of meditation available to all, which improves physical and mental health (by reducing stress); its origin is said to go back to Vedic times. Maharishi Mahesh Yogi also acquired from his guru, whom he reveres under the name Gur Dev, a good knowledge of the Hindu scriptures (he is also the author of a commentary on the Bhavagad Gita).

On the death of his guru, Maharishi Mahesh Yogi first spent two years in silence in his retreat in the Himalayas, and then went to South India, where he began to teach his technique. In 1958 in Madras he founded the World Movement for Spiritual Regeneration, which was a prelude to the mission he was to engage in in the West, according to legend in conformity to the wishes of his deceased guru. Seeing the spectacular results and benefits of his technique on the life of individuals and calculating, on his own account, that it would take more than two centuries at the existing rate of expansion to reach all humanity, he decide to go to the United States with its more rapid forms of communication. He undertook a first journey which led him to Burma, then to Kuala Lumpur, Singapore, Hong Kong and Hawaii, arriving in San Francisco in April 1959.

The movement then began to expand, first in the United States and then in Europe, benefiting from the support of several show-business personalities like the Beatles and Mia Farrow, who helped to make it known to the public. After the creation of the Students' International Meditation Society, the teaching of Transcendental Meditation reached the first campuses, and in 1967 Maharishi Mahesh Yogi gave lectures at Berkeley, Harvard, UCLA and Yale.

At the same time, through the creation of a network of organizations, associations and 'universities', often with pompous titles, the leaders of the movement gave Transcendental Meditation a base in a great variety of milieus. This raises questions about the real purpose of the movement, since the administrative and decision-making apparatus which it has developed on a world scale is too large simply to serve to secure the mental health of all humanity. In fact for some years Transcendental Meditation has been seeking to gain entry into the political scene. In 1989 it offered its services to President George Bush of the USA as a mediator over the hostage crisis in the Lebanon, and in 1990 it offered its services for resolving the crisis in the Gulf. In March 1992 it published a manifesto for a Natural Law Party in the British press which had many sections (the economy, tax, education and training, employment, health, social policy, law and order, defence, the environment and agriculture); similar parties have been created in France and Switzerland.

To see better the speculative framework of Transcendental Meditation, we need first to understand the specific sense that its founder gives to the adjective 'transcendental'. According to Maharishi Mahesh Yogi, 'transcendental' denotes something that 'goes beyond', and serves to define a technique of specific and natural meditation which leads those who practise it spontaneously beyond the usual level of their experience towards a state of profound repose, accompanied with a lively mind. He also uses the term to characterize the one eternal and non-manifest reality, which he calls Being or pure Being, the ultimate reality of creation, corresponding to the *brahman* of the Upanishads.

To explain the fundamental mechanism of Transcendental Meditation, Maharishi Mahesh Yogi uses an analogy, comparing the spirit to an ocean. Just as an ocean is disturbed on the surface by waves, so too the superficial levels of the spirit are active, since it is at their level that thoughts, emotions and perceptions are perceived as such. By contrast, the lower levels of the spirit remain silent and calm like the bed of the ocean. But what is the subtle link between the subconscious part (the lower levels) and the conscious part of the spirit? To answer this question Maharishi Mahesh Yogi resorts to the following image. The thoughts and emotions emanate from the subconscious part of the spirit like a bubble of air which rises from the bed of the ocean. Because of the enormous pressure at this depth, the bubble starts small and then increases as it rises to the surface. Similarly, when the thought-bubble is born in the profound depths of the spirit, its subtle states are not perceived. It is only when it is sufficiently developed, when it arrives at the level of the conscious spirit, that it is recognized as conscious thought.

Consequently the aim of Transcendental Meditation is to bring about an expansion of the conscious capacity of the spirit in its subconscious part so as to arrive at the conscious experience which is still at the subtle stages of its development in the subconscious. Thus Transcendental Meditation allows the attention to leave the active level of the spirit, and, turning it to some degree inwards, leads to a state of thought which is less and less developed. As the 'thought-bubbles' are produced in a continuous current, the spirit is led to have the experience of the bubble getting closer and closer to its origin. When attention reaches its source, it has crossed the whole depth of the spirit and attained the source of creative intelligence which is to be found in man.

According to Maharishi Mahesh Yogi, Transcendental Meditation allows the person meditating to attain a fourth state of consciousness, the state of 'transcendental consciousness' (the other three being the states of waking, dreaming and sleeping). This state is prolonged beyond the time of meditation itself, since the pure consciousness progressively increases, while the state of waking and activity decreases. The movement has drawn attention to the fact that scientific studies published in the United States in the 1970s showed that Transcendental Meditation has beneficial physiological and psychological effects, indicating that during meditation the subject is in a state of relaxation which can contribute to psychological balance and physical health. However, Maharishi Mahesh Yogi wants to go even further. He is persuaded that the beneficial effects of his technique will sooner or later extend from the individual to the whole of society and that Transcendental Meditation will be the spearhead of a great spiritual revolution. Hence the great hope that the movement places in the dissemination of his technique at the level of social and political institutions. The fact that Transcendental Meditation cannot be learned by an individual alone and needs the presence of a teacher also favours organized structures.

Bkaktivedanta Swami Prabhupada and Maharishi Mahesh Yogi represent two types of guru which have been exported from India. They are not the only ones. Of the many others mention might be made of Rajneesh Chandra Mohan (1931–1990), better known as Bhagwhan Shree Ranesh.

The Death of 'The Greatest Guru in the World'

RAJNEESH LEAVES 91 ROLLS-ROYCES

New Delhi, from our correspondent

Rajneesh is dead. He died on Friday 19 January, at 5.30 p.m., of a heart attack, in Pune, in the state of Maharashtra. He was the greatest guru in the world – at least for many hundreds of thousands or millions of his disciples. He also called himself Acharya, Bhagwan, Maitreyi Buddha, Zorba, and then at the end 'Osho', the 'Enlightened One'.

The death of Rajneesh is a cosmic, mystical, philosophical, psychedelic and sexual event, an event which it is feared a doubting West will mock. Rajneesh was probably a billionaire and he had a fleet of 91 Rolls-Royces; this was thought to be of no account. He had a long and superb white beard, a robe of precious material, a curious winter sports hat, a diamond watch and a heavy diamond bracelet. These were the wretched material things which basically he undoubtedly scorned.

So was Rajneesh mortal? Rajneesh, who 'gave birth' to so many unfortunates who had wallowed in ignorance before approaching him? Incredible! He had always said that death was the greatest joke, and burst out laughing. He is not dead; his teaching (zen, yoga, free love, sex without frontiers, pop psychology) happily survive him. Always with a twinkle in his eye, his hands joined, his orchestras of pop music, this was his message of love for all those who hated him across the world, from Australia to the Soviet Union, almost as many as those who adulated him.

Granted, twenty-two countries had refused him the right of residence, but one felt that these were on the point of changing their mind. Soon, the reign of Rajneesh, the love of Rajneesh, were going to envelop the world. The body of the 'Enlightened One' has been burned on a sandalwood pyre. His spirit is always present. But what is going to become of the Rolls-Royces?

(*Le Monde*, 21–22 January 1990)

3. The promise of 'interfaith dialogue': the experience of Dom Le Saux

Now that we have looked at the Hindu spiritual masters of the nineteenth and twentieth centuries and considered some of the gurus, real or supposed, who have come to the West to present particular facets of Hinduism, it seems appropriate to conclude this chapter with the exceptional spiritual adventure of a Christian, Fr Henri Le Saux (1910–1973). His attempt to live out in India a Hindu–Christian monasticism must be regarded as the basis of a new type of dialogue between the religions. Several years before Vatican II and its spirit of openness towards non-Christian religions, Dom Le Saux suggested a real dialogue based on personal experience involving faith, hope and love, a dialogue which, as he put it, can be summed up as the 'presence in one and the same heart of the Gospel and the Upanishads'.

Born in Brittany in 1910, the young Henry expressed his desire to become a priest at a very early age. After studying at the major seminary of Rennes, at the age of nineteen he entered the Benedictine abbey of Sainte Anne de Kergonan at Plouhamel. In 1934 he felt the call of India and the desire to establish there a monastic life inspired by the rule of St Benedict. In 1935 he took his final vows and was ordained priest in Vannes cathedral, thereafter teaching patristics and church history in his order. At the beginning of the Second World War he served in the French army; he was taken prisoner in 1940, but managed to escape and get back to his monastery. However, that was requisitioned by the Germans and the monks had to take refuge elsewhere until the end of the war.

In 1947, articles published in journals led to a correspondence between Dom Le Saux and Fr Jules Monchanin (1905–1957), who had been settled in India, in Tamil Nadu, since the middle of 1939 and was working in the diocese of Trichinopoly. As a result of this, Dom Le Saux secured permission from the abbot of his monastery to leave the community and go to India, where he arrived on

37. Frs Jules Monchanin (left) and Henri Le Saux with Bishop Mendoza

the Feast of the Assumption 1948. He made a deep impression on Fr Monchanin, and after a short stay in Trichinopoly the two men went to the presbytery in the town of Kulittalai where Monchanin was working. In January 1949, the two fathers went to the ashram of Ramana Maharshi for a *darshan* (vision = audience). This pilgrimage to Arunachala was to have a profound effect on the life of Fr Le Saux.

It seems that the two fathers had planned in December 1949 to organize the modest beginnings of an ashram in the spring of the following year at Tannirpalli, on the banks of the river Kaveri. On 21 March 1950, the Saccidananda Ashram, near to Kulittalai, came into being. At the time it consisted of two bamboo huts covered with coconut leaves, set in a wood of mango trees called Shantivanam ('wood of peace') by the fathers. Having been given leave by his parishioners, Fr Monchanin then began the life of a hermit in company with the Benedictine father. They put on the ochre robes of those who renounce life and adopted Indian names. Fr Monchanin thus became Swami Paramarubyanandam ('the bliss [*ananda*] of the supreme [*parama*] without form [*arapa*]' = the Holy Spirit), and Henri le Saux became Swami Abhishiktesvarananda (literally 'the bliss [*ananda*] of the anointed one [*abhishikta*] of the Lord [*isvara*]' = Christ) which he later abbreviated to Swami Abhishiktananda. Saccidananda, the name of the ashram, was also symbolic. It is formed of the terms *sat* ('being'), *cit* ('conscience') and *ananda* ('bliss'), which in non-dualistic Vedanta designate the three aspects or three proper names of the Absolute without attributes (*nirguna brahman*) on which the Hindu renunciant concentrates his mind to achieve deliverance (*moksha*). The fathers also emphasized that for the Christian monk this term takes on a new meaning, as an anticipation of the mystery of the trinitarian revelation.

In order to make their monastic ideal quite specific and to disarm in advance the critics of this experience of Hindu–Christian monasticism that there would certainly be, a long memorandum was published. It appeared on 11 October 1951, the date of the dedication of the chapel of the ashram, which was in Indian style, under the title *An Indian Benedictine Ashram*, and had the full support of the Bishop of Tiruchirapalli, Mgr Mendoza, who had written the preface. This support from their bishop was essential, since Indian Catholics had long been told that Hinduism was a satanic invention, and the training of the clergy was not at a sufficiently high theological or philosophical level to enable them to appreciate the intellectual and spiritual positions of the two fathers. By contrast, there were no problems in living in a Hindu milieu. There were fruitful exchanges with the Brahmins, the sadhus (ascetics) and the Buddhist religious.

Dom Le Saux had been deeply impressed by his first stay at Arunachala in January 1949 by the figure of R. Maharshi, and by the hymns that he heard sung in the ashram. He knew that he would return. In fact between 1949 and 1955, though basically residing at the Saccidananda Ashram, he made several retreats in the caves of Arunachala, the longest in 1952 (for five months). During these retreats, which had periods of silence but were punctuated by fruitful encounters with the sadhus or the Vedantic masters, Dom Le Saux saw the inner appeal of the Hindu mystical experience. He began to be profoundly torn between the experience of *advaita* (non-duality) – which constitutes the height of the experience of the Absolute (*nirguna brahman*) in Hindu mysticism – and a concern to remain faithful to Christ. His journal for the years 1952 to 1956 bears witness to the numerous dramas to which this led.

At the end of 1955, in Tirukoyilur, Dom Le Saux met Swami Gnanananda, a spiritual master whom he made his guru and with whom he stayed the following year. He regarded this encounter as a natural and indispensable complement to his monastic initiation and Hindu asceticism. The contact to some degree replaced the teaching that R. Maharshi departed too soon to be able to give him, and for which he had not been ready. In addition to this period with his guru in March, 1956 was also marked by a silent retreat from 5 November to 7 December in the Mauna Mandir of Kumbakonam (Tamil Nadu). During it he felt his psychological and physical limits. Though in his journal he recognized that he was not granted 'decisive illumination' nor even a definitive direction for his life, he described it as a 'milestone in his life'.

In his retreats in the caves of Arunachal and in the

Hindu temples, as also in contact with the masters and the sadhus, Dom le Saux encountered Hinduism at the level of rites and inner personal experience. This convinced him of their authenticity. He became persuaded that his vocation was to be a Hindu–Christian monk, and he believed that the church could only accomplish its mission in India if it encountered Indians at these same depths.

From this point on, the Saccidananda Ashram no longer seemed to correspond to the ideal of Swami Abhishiktananda. One only has to read his journal to note the gap which he saw between what he experienced at Arunachala or in the temples and what he felt at Shantivanam.

The two fathers, too different from one another, became increasingly remote from their original ideal and had taken different ways. Fr Monchanin found that it was impossible to fit Christianity into India and a few months before his death tried to explain why. He felt that basically the Hindus were not spiritually disquieted; they believed that they had supreme wisdom, so of what importance were the fluctuations or researches among those who had lesser wisdom? Christ was an avatar, and to Hindu eyes, while Christianity was a perfect morality, its metaphysics stopped short of the ultimate metamorphosis. Despite his attempt to make himself a Hindu among the Hindus, he also felt it impossible for a person to change culture, and realized that Christianity as such was part of his culture.

By contrast, at the end of his life Fr Le Saux, who had always put experience first, seems to have found the keys to what he called 'the marvellous solution to an equation', relating 'two forms of a single "faith"'. However, despite their different approach to India and their divergencies, the two fathers profoundly respected one another.

1957 was a key year for Dom le Saux. His co-founder of the Saccidananda Ashram returned to France, where he died of cancer, so Swami Abishiktananda resided only now and then at Shantivanam, though he continued to be interested in its future. However, he never returned after the ashram was taken over in 1968 by Fr Bede Griffiths, another important figure whose career unfortunately we cannot go into here. In 1959 he made his first pilgrimage to the Himalayas and became an Indian citizen the next year. Captivated by northern India, in 1961 he settled in a hermitage at Uttarkasi (Uttar Pradesh), a town on the Gangotri road which leads to the sources of the Ganges. From this date he divided his time between his Himalayan hermitage and very many journeys in India, to preach at retreats or to take part here and there in the work of the Indian church or ecumenical meetings. And until 1968 he kept returning to Shantinavam. He died on 7 December 1973, after a heart attack.

38. Henri Le Saux (1910–1973). A photograph taken in the last year of his life

Having built a bridge between East and West, Swami Abhishiktananda lived out to the depth of his being the experience of a synthesis between the quest for the Absolute in Indian fashion and the mystery of salvation revealed by Christ. His career was quite exceptional. This joint experience of *advaita* and Christianity, neither of which he ever denied, may pose problems to the theologian, but it is doubly prophetic. Not only does it open up perspectives for a Christian theology of non-Christian religions, but it still appears to be a formidable counter to integralisms or religious nationalisms in the recognition of the 'other' which it implies.

Conclusion

Among the Eastern religions (Buddhism, Hinduism, Taoism) which have attracted the interest of a Western public outside university circles for more than thirty years, Hinduism occupies a special place, above all for three reasons.

To begin with, it was historically the first of these three religions to be known to a wider public in the West. At a very early stage in Europe it benefited from the privileged support of the Theosophical Society, which from the end of the nineteenth century disseminated a number of Hindu religious or philosophical conceptions, and contributed towards propagating certain Hindu terms in esoteric or occultist circles.

At the same time, under the influence of a certain number of Hindu reformers and modern gurus, notably Swami Vivekananda, Hinduism was the first Eastern religion to become a universal religion. This is what is called the Hindu mission. This universal vocation also contributed towards giving a lasting place in the mind of the great Western public to an image of Hinduism shaped by the teachings of the neo-Hindu synthesis. Even today, this public is often no better informed about what Hinduism really is than the Theosophists were at the end of the last century. To confirm this, one only has to look at the pseudo-Orientalist literature on the shelves of bookshops, where they are to be found labelled 'esoteric', which is a feature of the 'New Age' literature.

Finally, the spread of the psychological and physiological techniques of Hinduism (yoga) from the first part of the twentieth century, and above all after the Second World War, have made the public familiar with other aspects of Hinduism, even if they have not always grasped its scope.

This type of approach to Hinduism, which can for many reasons be called 'Romantic', is still characteristic of the approach of a number of disabused Westerners confronted with the spectacle of the modern Western world and seeking another kind of experience. However, they often lack any knowledge of the cultural facts of the Hindu world, and for the most part are ignorant of their own religious tradition. Can they attain the sources of the riches of the Hindu tradition? Certainly contact with the East will allow Westerners to discover an inner dimension and even to regain the identity which they have lost. However, this can never be done at a superficial level. For a true knowledge of Hinduism much deeper dedication and commitment is needed. That is why Dom Le Saux is such an important figure and forms a fitting end this study. Hinduism can never be a hobby of Westerners. The real dialogue with India is a difficult way which demands the total renunciation of the self.

The Meaning of Dialogue

If one sees only the surface, like certain tourists and journalists, then the whole of Hinduism could be dismissed as superstition and nonsense. But the surface is misleading; there is so much pure gold in the soil, once one begins to dig. And it is our task to unearth this gold. 'Dialogue' is not only the registering of each visible phenomenon; dialogue is creative in itself, it is a release. Only in the dialogue does a Hindu learn the essence of Hinduism, and the Christian find the essence of Christianity. Just as important as the 'external' dialogue, the encounter with the non-Christian in conversation, is the 'inner' dialogue, the debate with the essence of Hinduism in our own hearts. There the decisions are taken; there new insights are gained.

He who has understood the meaning of the dialogue will not want to have anything more to do with academic dalliance or a science of comparative religion, behaving as if it stood above all religions. He will also not want to know anything more of a certain kind of theology that works 'without presuppositions' and pleases itself in manipulating definitions and formulas and forgets about man, who is the main concern. He will be more and more pulled into what I called 'spirituality': the real life of the mind. I wanted to see a famous man in Benares, a sagacious philosopher, feared by many as a merciless critic of Christian theology. I had my own reasons for paying him a visit. He was polite, invited me for tea and then mounted the attack. I let him talk his fill, without saying a word myself. Then I started to talk about the things I had begun to understand within the dialogue – quite positively Christian. We got into a sincere, good, deep discussion. He had intended to send me away after ten minutes. When I left after two hours he had tears in his eyes: 'If we insisted on our theologies – you as a Christian, I as a Hindu – we should be fighting each other. We have found one another because we probed more deeply, towards spirituality.'

(Klaus Klostermaier, *Hindu and Christian in Vrindaban*, 98–9)

39. The largest Hindu temple outside India, Neasden, London

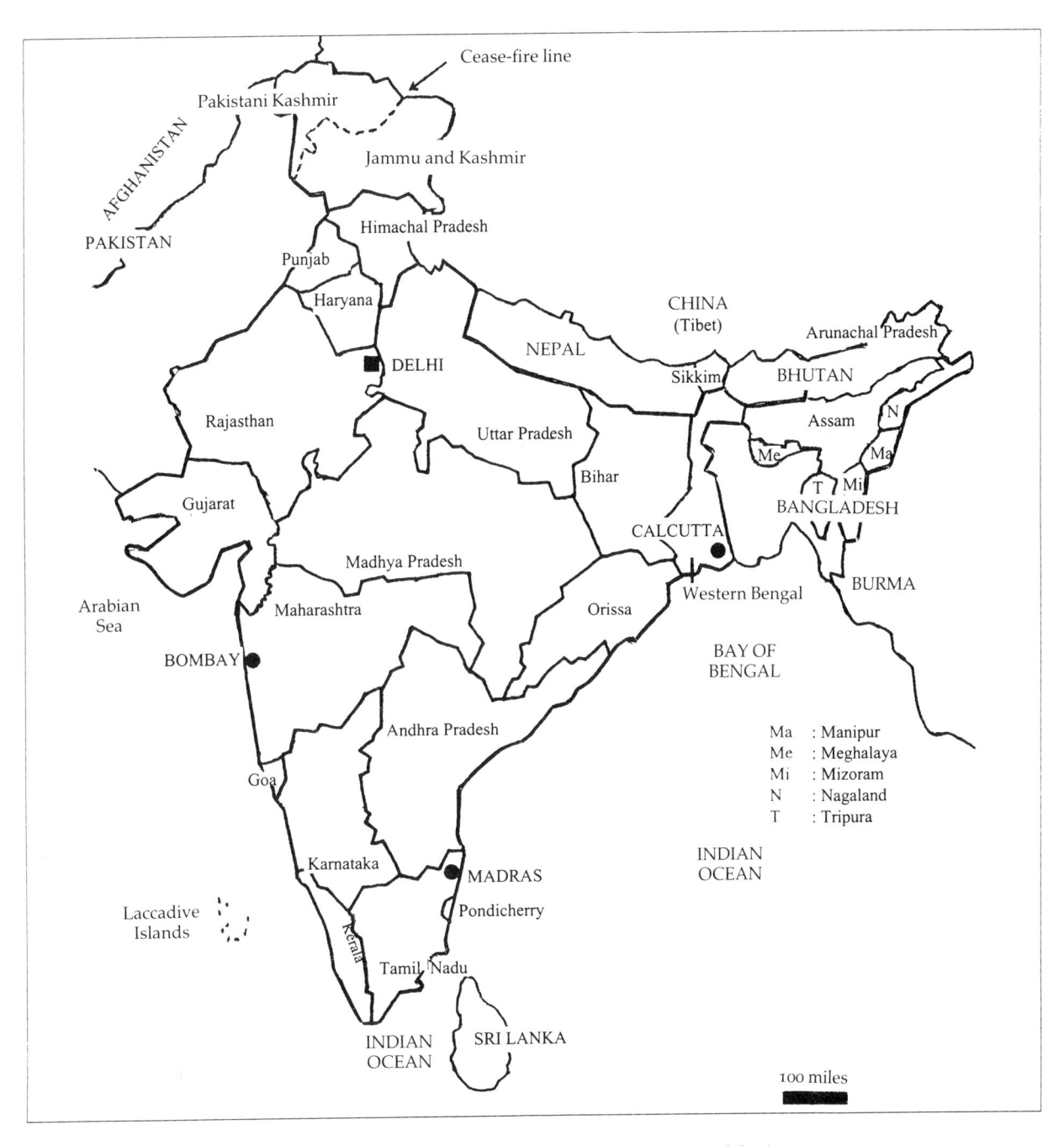

The Indian Union (simplified Administrative Map)

For Further Reading

Texts

Convenient editions of many of the Hindu texts mentioned in this book (or extracts from them) are available as Penguin Classics. They also contain further detailed bibliographies. See e.g.

The Bhagavad Gita, edited by Juan Mascaró, 1962
Hindu Myths, edited by Wendy Doniger O'Flaherty, 1975
The Laws of Manu, edited by Wendy Doniger O'Flaherty with Brian K. Smith, 1991
The Rig Veda, edited by Wendy Doniger O'Flaherty, 1981
The Upanishads, edited by Juan Mascaró, 1970

For the Upanishads, see also the classic translation edited by F. Max Müller, *The Upanishads* (two vols, 1879, 1884), reissued by Dover Books 1962, now showing its age but conveniently accessible. Also R. E. Hume, *The Thirteen Principal Upanishads*, Oxford University Press ²1934

There are many retellings of the Mahabharata and the Ramayana; attractive versions at a reasonable length are those by Kamala Subramaniam, Bharatiya Vidya Bhavan, Bombay 1965, 1981

See also:

Hemant Kanitkar, *The Hindu Scriptures*, Heinemann 1994

On the history of India

John Marshall, *Mohenjo-Daro and the Indus Civilization*, Probsthain 1931
Francis Watson, *A Concise History of India*, Thames and Hudson 1974 (with illustrations)
Mortimer Wheeler, *The Indus Civilization*, Cambridge University Press ³1968

For basic reference, in addition to the many dictionaries on world religions

John Dowson, *A Classical Dictionary of Hindu Mythology and Religion*, Rupa and Co, Calcutta, Allahabad, Bombay and New Delhi 1982
A Brief Dictionary of Hinduism, Vedanta Press 1962

On Hinduism generally

P. Bowes, *The Hindu Religious Tradition*, Routledge 1978
V. P. (Hemant) Kanitkar and W. Owen Cole, *Teach Yourself Hinduism*, Hodder Headline and NTC Publishing Group, Lincolnwood 1995
David R. Kinsley, *Hinduism*, Prentice-Hall 1982
John M. Koller, *The Indian Way*, Macmillan 1982
Sarvepalli Radhakrishnan and Charles A. Moore, *A Source Book in Indian Philosophy*, Princeton University Press 1957
Krishna Sivaraman (ed.), *Hindu Spirituality. Vedas through Vedanta*, Crossroad Publishing Company and SCM Press Ltd 1989
R. C. Zaehner, *Hinduism*, Oxford University Press 1966

On modern movements in Hinduism

Ronald Duncan (ed.), *The Writings of Gandhi*, Fontana Books 1971
M. K. Gandhi, *An Autobiography* (also published as *Gandhi: My Experiments with Truth*), Jonathan Cape 1949
Kim Knott, *My Sweet Lord. The Hare Krishna Movement*, Aquarian Press 1986
P. Mason, *The Maharishi*, Element Books 1994
R. McDermott (ed.), *The Essential Aurobindo*, Lindisfarne Press 1991
A. Osborne (ed.), *The Teachings of Ramana Maharshi*, Century 1962
L. D. Shinn, *The Dark Lord. Cult Images and the Hare Krishnas in America*, Westminster Press 1987

On Hindu-Christian dialogue

Klaus Klostermaier, *Hindu and Christian in Vrindaban*, SCM Press 1969, reissued 1993
J. Monchanin and H. le Saux, *A Benedictine Ashram*, Times Press 1964
Murray Rogers, *Christian Ashram*, Darton, Longman and Todd 1966
Murray Rogers, *Marriage of East and West*, Collins 1982
M. M. Thomas, *The Acknowledged Christ of the Indian Renaissance*, SCM Press 1970

List of Boxes

1. The Vedic Upanishads 10
2. The Three Social Functions and the Caste System; Caste 12
3. Varuna 15
4. Indra 16
5. Agni 17
6. The Preparation of Soma 18
7. Usas 20
8. Indra slays Vrtra 22
9. Three Cosmogonies from the Rig Veda 24
10. 'You are That, Svetaketu' 30–1
11. The Self and Immortality 40
12. Disinterested Action 44
13. The Attainment of Deliverance 45
14. In Praise of Krishna 45
15. The Mahabharata 46
16. The Ramayana 48
17. The Scheme of Avatars 61
18. What is Vedanta? 76
19. The Laws of Manu 77
20. The Idea of 'Reincarnation' for Non-Hindus 78
21. India and the Cult of the Cow 81
22. The Hindu Calendar 83
23. The 'Ayodhya Affair' 88
24. The Teaching of Ramakrishna 94
25. Gandhi 97
26. Ramana Maharshi on Death and Immortality 98
27. The Teaching of Sri Aurobindo 100
28. The Death of 'The Greatest Guru in the World' 105
29. The Meaning of Dialogue 111

List of Illustrations

*Figure drawings by Ian Cargill
and Victor Davidson*

1. The Indus valley, showing the centres of Harappa and Mohenjo-Daro 3
2. Terracotta statuette of female deity from the Indus valley 4
3. 'Lord of the beasts' 4
4. The 'great bath' of Mohenjo-Daro, with ancillary buildings (reconstruction) 5
5. Bull found on a seal from Mohenjo-Daro 6
6. Rudra, storm god of the Vedas 14
7. Apsaras (heavenly dancer) 20
8. Naga and Nagini (snake deities) 21
9. Sandstone Yaksha 21
10. Agni, represented as a figure with two heads 53
11. Ganesha, elephant-headed with his shakti (consort) 54
12. Ganesha at Hoysalesvara temple 55
13. Durga slaying buffalo demon 56
14. Kali 57
15. Brahma at Huccappyagudi temple 58
16. Brahma the creator, facing four directions 59
17. Lord Vishnu and his attributes 59
18. Vishnu reclining on the serpent Ananta 60
19. Vishnu with his tortoise avatar at the churning of the ocean 62
20. Vishnu's three strides and his dwarf avatar 63
21. Krishna dancing on the defeated serpent Kaliya 64
22. Infant Balakrishna 65
23. Krishna Gopala playing his flute 65
24. Krishna the divine herdsman, playing the flute 66
25. Bhairava: Shiva in his terrible form 67
26. Shiva as Bhairava with skulls 67
27. Triune image of Shiva as the great god 68
28. Shiva contemplating as the master of all wisdom 68
29. Shiva Natarja – Lord of the dance 69
30a. Shiva linga at the sanctuary of Gudimallam 70
30b. Shiva Natarja 70
31. Shiva and his consort Parvati on a lotus flower 71
32. Linga and Yoni 72
33. Ramakrishna (1836–1886) 95
34. Swami Vivekananda (1863–1902) 96
35. Ramana Maharshi (1879–1950) 98
36. Ma Ananda Mayi (1896–1982) 101
37. Frs Jules Monchanin and Henri le Saux with Bishop Mendoza 106
38. Henri Le Saux (1910–1973) 108
39. The largest Hindu temple outside India, Neasden, London 112

Index and Glossary

Abishiktananda, Swami (*see* Le Saux, Henri)
Adibrahma Samaj, 90
Adityas, 13, 14, 19, 46, 56
Advaita (non-dualism), 29, 76, 93
Agni, 8, 14, 17, 18, 19, 29, 23, 25, 26, 33, 34, 47, 54, 61
Agnistoma (eulogy to Agni), 34
ahimsa (absence of desire to kill), 66, 80, 97
Alfassa, Mirra, 99
Allah Unpanishad, 42
Amsha, 13
ananda (absolute happiness), 28
Ananta, 59, 60, 84
Apsaras, 20, 62
Aranyakas, 9, 39
Arjuna, 44, 45, 46, 47, 61, 65
Aryaman, 13
Aryan, Aryans, 3, 4, 5, 6, 7, 11, 17, 92
Arya Samaj, 89, 92, 93
ashrama (stage of life), viii, 43
Asuras, 14, 15, 63, 65
Asvins (*Asvini devatas*), 11, 13, 46
Atharva Vedea, 8, 9, 55f.
atman (self), 9, 25, 27, 28, 29, 35, 39, 75, 101
Armya Sabha, 90
Aurobindo Ghose, Sri, 47, 98, 99, 100
Auroville, 99
Avatar, 45, 59, 61, 62ff.
Ayodhya, 47, 83, 85, 86, 87, 88

Balakrishna, 64
Bali, 63, 84
Banerji, Rakhal Das, 3
Bhagavad Gita, 12, 44, 47, 61, 65, 76, 79
Bhairava, 67
Bhaja, 13
bhakti (devotion), 39, 42, 45, 47, 52, 63, 79, 86, 103
bhakti-marga (way of devotion), 42
bhakti-yoga, 45, 46
Bhaktivedanta, A.C., 65
Bhave, V., 96
Blavatsky, Helena Petrovna, ix
Brahma, 44, 53, 56, 57, 62, 63, 68, 71, 73, 77, 85
brahmachari (one who cultivates *brahman*), 33
brahmacharya (period of study), viii
brahman (impersonal Absolute), viii, 7, 9, 26, 27, 28, 29, 39, 40, 41, 57, 73, 79, 90, 93, 101
Brahmanas, 8, 9, 13, 14, 26, 27, 28, 29, 39, 43, 58
brahmanda ('egg of Brahma'), 73
Brahmanism, 52, 53, 87
Brahma Samaj, 90, 93, 95
Brahma Sutras, 76
Brahmin, viii, 11, 12, 15, 28, 33, 39, 40, 63, 76, 81
Brihadarankya Upanishad, 10, 13, 27, 41, 75
Brihaspati, 57
Buddha, Gautama, 66

Calendar, 82f.

Caste, 5, 11
Chaitanya, Sri Krishna, 65, 87, 91, 102
chakra ('wheel'), 50
Chandogya Upanishad, 9, 10, 30f., 41, 75
cit (consciousness), 28, 107
Cow, sacred, 81

daitya, 63
Daksha, 13
darshana (perspective on the real), 41, 53, 86
Dasas, 5
Dasgupta, S., 96
Dasyus, 5, 17, 92
De, Abhay Charan, 102, 103
dharma, viii, 42, 43, 47, 59, 61, 66, 73, 79
Dharma Shastras, 10, 41, 43
Dumézil, Georges, 11
Durga, 51, 56, 84, 91
dvapara yuga (age characterized by two), 73f.
Dyasupita, 14, 19

Eliade, Mircea, 52

Ganesha, 55, 84
Gandhi, Mahatma, 86, 97
Ganges, 5, 40, 86
Ganharvas, 20
guna (attribute), 57, 60, 73
Griffiths, Bede, 87, 108
Guru, 33, 42, 53, 79
Guru Nanak, 87

Hanuman, 47, 55, 83
Harappa, 3, 4
Harivansa, 43, 64, 84
Hiranyaksha, 62, 63
Hiranyakashipu, 63
hiranya garbha (golden embryo), 16, 23
Holi, 84
hotr (priest), 8

Indra, 8, 11, 13, 14, 16, 17, 19, 20, 22, 23, 25, 53, 54, 58
Indus, viii, 3, 5

International Society for Krishna Consciousness (ISKCON), 65, 102f.
ishta, devata (chosen deity), 45, 53

Jagganath, 84
Jesus, 90, 91, 94
jiva (soul), 75
jivanmukta (living delivered one), 79
jnana (intuition), 26
jnana yoga, 46

Kabir, 87
Kali, 93
kali yuga (evil age), 64, 66
Kalki, 66
kalpa (world cycle), 73
Kalpa Sutras, 29
Kama, 85
kama (desire), viii, 23
karma, 26, 27, 55, 75, 77, 79, 101
karma yoga, 46
Krishna, 44, 45, 46, 47, 56, 61, 74, 67, 74, 84, 94, 102
krita yuga (age accomplished), 73
Kshatriyas, 11, 12, 15, 33, 44, 63, 64, 76
Kubera, 55, 56
Kumbh Mela, 85f.
Kundalini, 50
Kurma, 62

Lakshmi, 56, 62, 85
Le Saux, Henri, 87, 106ff., 110
linga, 68, 71, 85

Mahabharata, 10, 11, 41, 43, 44, 46, 72
Mahadevan, T., 96
Maharishi Mahesh Yogi, 103, 104
Maharshi, Ramana, 42, 96, 98, 100, 106, 107
mahatman (supreme self), 41
maha yuga (great age), 73f.
Maharaj, Sri Nisargadadath, 101
Maitri Upanishad, 42
manas (consciousness, thought), 23
Mandala, 51
Mandukya Upanisahad, 10, 29

Mantra, 50
Manu, 25, 43, 62
   Laws of, 43, 74, 77
Marshall, Sir John, 3, 4, 72
Maruts, 16, 46, 55
Matysa, 62
Mayi, Ma Ananda, 100
Meru, Mount, 73
Mirabai, 87
Misra, Visvambhara, 65
Mitra, 11, 13, 14, 15, 19, 54
Mohenjo-Daro, 3, 4, 72
moksha (deliverance), viii, 26, 45, 50, 68, 72, 79, 101
Monchanin, Jules, 87, 106ff.
Muhammad, 42, 94
Muktika Upanishad, 42
Müller, F. Max, 13, 95
Mundaka Upanishad, 10, 29

Nagas (snake gods), 7, 20, 21
Nakta, 19
Narasimha, 63, 83
Nasatyas (*see also* Asvins), 13, 20, 34
Nataraja, 68
Natural Law Party, 104
Noble, Margaret, 95

Olcott, Henry Steel, ix

Pabhupada, Swami (*see* Bhaktivedanta, A.C.)
pancaratra (dissolution), 59, 66
Parliament of the World's Religions ix, 95
Parasurama, 63, 64
Parvati, 56, 71
Pasupati ('lord of the beasts'), 4, 13, 67, 72
Prajapati, 13, 22, 25, 33, 57, 58
Prajnapad, Swami, 101
prakrti (fundamental nature), 72, 73, 74, 75
pralaya (dissolution), 59, 66, 73
prana (breath), 75
prasada (divine grace), 45, 79
Prithivimata, 19
puja (rite), 81, 82
punya (merit), 75, 79

Puranas, 10, 41, 49, 50, 52, 62, 64, 66, 67, 68
Purusha, 23, 25
purusha (spirit), 57, 61, 71, 75
Pushan, 19

Radakrishnan, S., 96
Radha, 56
Rai, Govinda, 94
rajas ('dust'), 57
Rajneesh Chandra Mohan, 105
Rakshashas, 22, 47, 64
Rama, 47, 48, 49, 55, 63, 64, 83, 85, 88, 97
Ramakrishna, 42, 87, 93, 94, 96, 101
Ramakrishna Mission, ix, 96, 101
Ramakrishna Upanishad, 42
Ramayana, 10, 41, 43, 47, 48, 49, 55, 88, 97
Ranadasa, Swami, 100
Rati, 56
Rbhus, 20
Reincarnation, 78
Rig Veda, 8, 9, 12, 14, 15, 16, 18, 19, 23, 27, 28, 33, 43, 55, 72
rishis (sages), 7, 8, 13
Roy, Ram Mohan, 87, 89, 90, 93
Rudra, 13, 14, 16, 46, 47
Rudra Shiva, 42

Sama Veda, 8, 9, 28
Samanyavedanta Upanishads, 41
Samhitas, 8, 9, 27, 51
Samkhya, 72, 79
Samnyasi Upanishads, 42
samsara (cycle of rebirth), viii, 26, 27, 61
samskara (purification rite), 32, 43
Sankar, Mull (*see* Sarasvati, Dayananda)
Sankara, 47, 76
sankhya, 56, 57
sannyasa (renunciation), viii, 47, 50, 79
santana dharma (eternal law), viii
Sarasvati, 85, 86
Sarasvati, Swami Baktisiddhanta, 103
Sarasvati, Dayananda, 91, 92
Sarasvati, Swami Sivananda, 100f.
Sarasvati, Swami Virjananda, 91

Satapatha Brahmana, 9, 15, 23, 32, 62
sattva, 57
Savitri, 19
Sen, Keshab Chandra, 90, 91, 94
Sesha (*see* Ananta)
Shakti, 50, 56, 84
Shiva, 4, 7, 13, 41, 50, 53, 56, 57, 66f., 72, 83, 88, 91
Shudras, 11, 12
sisna (phallus), 7
Skanda, 55, 56
smrti, 10, 30, 47, 86
Soma, 8, 16, 17, 18, 19, 20, 23, 33, 34, 35, 43, 54, 62
sraddha (trust), 30, 33
srauta (solemn rite), 32, 33
srishti (emanation), 73
sruti, 7, 8, 9, 10, 30, 47
Sur-Das, 87
Surya, 19
Svetasvatara Upanishad, 10, 41, 42, 67

Tagore, Devednranath, 90
Tagore, Dvarkanath, 90
Tagore, Rabindranath, 96
Taittiriya Upanishad, 10, 29
Tantras, Tantrism, 41, 50, 51, 52, 79, 93
tapas (creative ardour), 23, 72
tat tvam asi ('you are that'), 9, 28, 30f.
Theosophical Society, ix, 101, 110
Transcendental Meditation, 104, 105
treta yuga (age of triad), 73
trimurti (trinity), 57, 60, 66
Tulsi-Das, 49, 87
Tvastr, 20, 25

Ulladu Narpadu, 42
Upanishads, 9, 10, 25, 26, 27, 29, 39, 44, 52, 74, 76

Usas, 19, 20

vach (word), 7, 50, 85
Vaishyas, 11, 12, 14, 76
Vallabha, 87
Valmiki, 43, 49
Vamana, 63
Varaha, 62
varna (caste), viii, 11, 25, 43, 58
Varuna, 8, 11, 13, 14, 15, 23, 54
Vasus, 13, 46
Vayu, 11, 19, 25, 28, 54, 55, 61
Veda, 7ff., 41, 46
Vedanta, ix, 9, 75, 79, 95
Vedavyasa, 8, 83
vedi (altar), 33
vibhabva (manifestation), 61
vibhuti (manifestation), 59, 61
Vishnu, 41, 49, 53, 56, 57, 58, 61ff., 68, 71, 72, 74, 83, 85, 88, 102
Visvakarma, 20, 25, 57
Vivekananda, Swami, ix, 87, 95, 96, 110
Vrindaban, 84, 103
Vrtra, 16, 17, 18, 20, 22, 54, 58
Vrtrahatya (killing of Vrtra), 16
Vyasa, 49
vyuha (emanation), 59, 60

Yajur Veda, 8, 9, 13, 28, 33
yajus (sacrificial formula), 8, 25
Yakshas, 7, 20, 21, 55
Yama, 25, 26, 54, 55
Yami, 15
Yoga, 42, 45, 72, 79, 110
Yoga Upanishads, 42
yoni (vulva), 71, 72
yuga (world age), 58, 72, 73f.